A Taste of the 18th Century

By Paxson Collins MacDonald
and Cynthia Marie Conte

Published by
Michie Tavern *ca.* 1784
683 Thomas Jefferson Parkway
Charlottesville, Virginia 22902
www.michietavern.com

Recipe compilation by Paxson Collins MacDonald
History by Cynthia Marie Conte
Cover and book design by Serelda Elliott
Cover photography by Philip Beaurline
e-mail comments to info@michietavern.com

Library of Congress Catalog Card Number: 99-74156
ISBN: 0-9672351-0-3

Printed in the United States of America
Toof Cookbook Division

Toof Commercial Printing
670 South Cooper Street
Memphis, TN 38104

Acknowledgements

A Taste of the 18th Century is a compilation of recipes that date back to the 1700s. Many of the recipes have been updated so that you may prepare them at home. To keep them authentic, we do not include any prepared foods in the ingredients. We would like to thank all of our friends who provided their sacred family recipes, especially Josie Conte, Matalie Griffin Deane, June Chaffin, Laurel Mull, Susan Jane Collins, Elizabeth Stargell, Katie Lou Webb, long-gone chefs from Mr. Michie's kitchen, present-day chefs in Michie Tavern's kitchen and many aunts, uncles, and cousins of the aforementioned who kept the kitchen hearth fire burning. —PCM

Table of Contents

 Recipes from *The Ordinary*

Recipes from Yuletide Dinners

ICHIE TAVERN, a Virginia Historic Landmark, is one of the oldest homesteads remaining in Virginia. Time and the forces of Mother Nature have been good to this homestead and by way of grace, hard work and much love, the Inn now stands well preserved on a mountain in Charlottesville, near Thomas Jefferson's beloved Monticello.

The Museum, rich in folklore and history, offers visitors a glimpse into the past, and The Ordinary still serves hot meals to weary travelers.

So turn the pages of history back and journey to colonial Virginia. We've collected a treasury of southern, traditional recipes that will be enjoyed by your family today—experience *a taste of the 18th century.*

The Ordinary

BILL OF FARE
May change seasonally

Colonial Fried Chicken

Murphy's Biscuits

Michie Tavern Corn Bread

Black-eyed Peas ∿ Green Bean Salad

Southern Beets ∿ Stewed Tomatoes

Cole Slaw ∿ Potato Salad

Garden Vegetable Soup

Crispy Peach Cobbler

Author's note–
We have made every effort to ensure that these recipes, when
prepared at home, will taste like the authentic foods at Michie Tavern
but please understand that we order special ingredients and cook in
deep fryers and convection ovens. Also, since we prepare our dishes
in bulk, it is sometimes difficult to transcribe these recipes
into much smaller portions. Thank you.

 *Colonial Fried Chicken*

1 cup all-purpose flour

1 teaspoon oregano

1 teaspoon garlic salt

1 teaspoon seasoning salt

1 teaspoon pepper

2- to 3-pound fryer, cut up

3 cups shortening

Combine flour and seasonings; roll the cut up chicken in the flour mixture. Using a Dutch oven or other heavy deep pan, fry in shortening at 350° for 12 to 15 minutes on each side, or until tender.

Yield: 6 servings

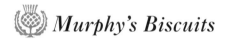 *Murphy's Biscuits*

2 cups all-purpose flour

2 teaspoons baking powder

¼ teaspoon salt

3 tablespoons shortening

⅔ cup whole milk

Sift together flour, baking powder and salt. Cut in shortening and then stir in milk quickly with fork to make dough light and fluffy but not sticky. Knead until dough is smooth, approximately 10 times. Roll out the dough on lightly floured board. Cut into biscuits ½-inch thick. Bake on greased cookie sheet at 450° for 8 to 10 minutes.

Yield: 10 to 12 biscuits

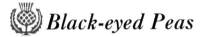 Michie Tavern Corn Bread

2 cups self-rising white stone
   ground corn meal
½ cup sugar

¾ cup milk
2 eggs
½ cup canola oil

Sift together corn meal and sugar in a large bowl. Add milk, eggs and oil.
Stir with a wooden spoon just until all ingredients are wet and smooth. Bake
in a greased 8-inch square pan in preheated oven at 425° for 15–20 minutes.
Cut into squares and serve. Note: To achieve Michie Tavern's same
consistency and crunchiness, use the exact corn meal suggested here.

Yield: 9 to 12 servings

 Black-eyed Peas

1 pound fresh black-eyed peas
1 ham hock or 1 slice salt pork

1 teaspoon pepper
1 tablespoon butter or margarine

Rinse the peas thoroughly; strain. In a large pot, add the peas and pork with
enough water to cover. Cook for 50 minutes or until the peas are tender.
Gently mix in the pepper and butter.

Yield: 4 to 6 servings

Marinated Green Bean Salad

1-pound can green beans
   that are cut and firm
½ cup vinegar
½ cup salad oil

2 tablespoons sugar
2 teaspoons garlic salt
1½ teaspoon ground oregano
1 teaspoon pepper

Drain beans and set aside. In a large bowl combine all other ingredients and
whisk well. Add the beans, gently stir and chill for one hour. Before serving,
stir to distribute marinade.

Yield: 4 to 6 servings

 Mrs. Michie's Southern Beets

1 pound fresh beets	3 tablespoons water
¼ cup sugar	¾ of a small onion (diced)
¼ cup vinegar	Salt and pepper to taste

Boil beets approximately one hour (depending on size), skin, slice and set aside. (If canned beets are used, include juices and eliminate water.) Combine sugar, vinegar and water; then add beets, diced onion, salt and pepper. Cover and marinate in refrigerator about eight hours.

Yield: 4 to 6 servings

 Stewed Tomatoes

4 cups canned tomatoes, quartered	2 tablespoons butter, melted
½ cup sugar	Salt, pepper to taste
	6 baked biscuits

Mix together the tomatoes, sugar, butter and salt. Crumble the biscuits and add to the mixture. Cover and cook in saucepan over medium heat for 15 minutes.

Yield: 6 servings

Cole Slaw

¼ cup vinegar	1 small firm cabbage, shredded
¼ cup sugar	1 medium carrot, grated
⅓ cup mayonnaise	

In a small dish, combine the vinegar, sugar and mayonnaise; stir until the sugar is dissolved. Mix the cabbage and carrots in a large bowl. Pour the dressing over the vegetables. Mix and serve.

Yield: 6 to 8 servings

 # *Potato Salad*

6 large potatoes

1 tablespoon celery seed or
  ½ stalk celery, finely minced

¼ cup sugar

1 cup mayonnaise

1 teaspoon salt

1 small onion, diced

1 whole sweet pimento, diced

1 teaspoon pepper

⅓ cup prepared mustard

1 cup sweet relish or
  1 sweet pickle, diced

Dice the potatoes and cook until tender. Drain, rinse with cold water and drain again. Add celery. Let cool for one hour. Mix together the remaining ingredients; stir gently into the diced potatoes.

Yield: 6 to 8 servings

 # *Garden Vegetable Soup*

2 tablespoons canola oil

2 cloves fresh garlic, diced

1 diced onion

½ cup diced carrots

½ cup diced green pepper

½ cup diced celery

6 cups chicken broth

15 ounces crushed tomatoes

2 tablespoons tomato paste

1 cup cut green beans

2 medium diced potatoes

dash of ground red pepper

freshly ground black pepper

1 cup shredded cabbage (optional)

Heat oil in large stock pot. Briefly sauté garlic then add onions, carrots, peppers, and celery. Cook until softened. Add broth, crushed tomatoes (with juice), and tomato paste and bring to boil. Add remaining ingredients (including cabbage, if desired). If there is not enough broth, add water until desired thickness. Return to boil. Turn down heat and simmer until all vegetables are soft.

Yield: 8 servings

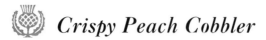

Crispy Peach Cobbler

BATTER

1 tablespoon softened butter

¼ cup sugar

1 teaspoon vanilla

1 egg, beaten

½ cup flour

½ cup milk

TOPPING

½ cup brown sugar

2 tablespoons melted butter

2 tablespoons sugar

2 tablespoons flour

1 cup oats

3 cups sliced peaches

To make batter, cream butter and sugar with mixer in small bowl. Add remaining ingredients and mix well. Set aside. To make topping, mix all ingredients except oats. Add those last and stir until mixed. Butter 2-quart casserole. Pour in batter. Spoon peaches gently on top but do not stir. Sprinkle topping over mixture evenly. Bake at 350° for 45–60 minutes until topping begins to brown and batter is set.

Yield: 6–8 servings

Note: If using fresh peaches, peel, slice and simmer in saucepan over low heat until peaches are tender. You may add 1/4 cup sugar if peaches are not ripe.

Beverages

Southerner's Mint Julep

8 dozen fresh mint leaves

8 teaspoons confectioners sugar

8 teaspoons water

8 tall glasses

2 cups bourbon

Crushed ice

8 sprigs fresh mint

Chill the glasses on ice in the refrigerator for at least 6 hours. In a medium-size mixing bowl, crush the mint leaves; mix in the sugar and water until the sugar is dissolved. Mix in 2 cups bourbon. Pour the mixture through a strainer. Discard the crushed mint leaves. Pack the glasses with crushed ice. Using a ladle, evenly pour the mixture over the crushed ice in each glass. Garnish each drink with a sprig of mint and serve.

Yield: 8 servings

Holiday Eggnog

12 eggs, separated

4 cups confectioners' sugar

4 cups dark rum, brandy, or
  bourbon or a combination
  of the three

2 quarts whipping cream

8–12 egg whites

3 teaspoons freshly-grated nutmeg

In a large bowl or punch bowl, beat egg yolks, added one at a time, until light in color. Gradually beat in sugar and then 2 cups of liquor. Cover mixture and let stand for one hour. Beating constantly, add 2 more cups of liquor and the whipping cream. Refrigerate covered for 3 hours. Beat egg whites until stiff and gently fold into the eggnog. Sprinkle with nutmeg and serve.

Yield: 24 servings

Note: For a less potent eggnog, the amount of liquor may be reduced.

Hot Buttered Rum

2 tablespoons confectioners sugar
1¼ cups water, boiling
2¾ cups rum

7 teaspoons butter, melted
Nutmeg to taste
6 cinnamon sticks

Warm 6 glasses in hot water. Dissolve sugar in boiling water. Stir in rum and butter. Pour into the heated tumblers. Garnish with the nutmeg and cinnamon stick.

Yield: 6 servings

Apple Toddy

1¼ cups rum
10½ cups apple brandy
6¼ cups boiling water
10 tablespoons sugar
1 dozen baked apples

6 dozen cloves
6 dozen allspice
11 sticks cinnamon
4 teaspoons nutmeg

Combine all of the ingredients in a large pot. Cover and store in a cool place for 6 days. Simmer over medium-low heat until very hot. Pour into mugs and serve.

Yield: 20 to 24 servings

Hot Spiced Apple Cider

9 cups apple juice or cider
8 medium sticks cinnamon
10 allspice

18 cloves
1 lemon rind, grated
8 jiggers rum

Combine all of the ingredients except for the rum. Boil for 5 minutes; reduce the heat, adding the rum. Cover and simmer over very low heat for another 5 minutes. Serve after straining.

Yield: 8 servings

Yankee Cobbler

2 dozen seedless grapes, halved
10 maraschino cherries, halved
Orange extract
16 jiggers whiskey

8 teaspoons sugar dissolved in
6 teaspoons boiling water
(allowed to cool)
2 oranges, sliced

Shave enough ice to fill 8 tall glasses. Mix in the grapes and cherries. Add the ice and fruit mix to the glasses; add a dash of orange extract to each. Combine the whiskey with the sugar solution. Pour evenly over the ice in each glass. Garnish each drink with 2 to 3 orange slices.

Yield: 8 servings

Cool 'n' Dizzy Flip

8 eggs
16 ounces wine or 8 ounces rum

8 teaspoons confectioners sugar
dissolved in 4 teaspoons water

With an electric mixer, blend all at high speed for 2 minutes. Pour into tall glasses over 3 to 4 ice cubes. Garnish with nutmeg to taste.

Yield: 8 servings

Strawberry Bracers

6 cups red wine
6 cups crushed strawberries

¾ cup sugar
6 teaspoons lemon juice

With an electric mixer, blend all of the ingredients at high speed for 2 minutes. Chill for ½ hour. Fill 6 tall glasses halfway with tonic water. Add an ice cube to each glass. Evenly pour the strawberry mixture into each glass and serve.

Yield: 6 servings

Original Regent Punch

1 pint strong tea

4 cups sugar

juice of 6 lemons

rind of 4 lemons

juice of 6 oranges

1 pint brandy

1 pint rum

2 quarts champagne

Mix tea with sugar until sugar is dissolved. Add next five ingredients and chill. Add chilled champagne when ready to serve.

Yield: 30 drinks

Today's Regent Punch

1 gallon tea

1 cup sugar

2 quarts orange juice

2 quarts lemonade

lemon and orange slices

Mix tea with sugar until sugar is dissolved. Add juices and chill. Serve with lemon and orange slices.

Yield: 30 drinks

Rose Petal Wine

1 quart of fresh pink rose petals*

2 cakes compressed yeast

1 gallon boiling water

6 cups sugar

Pack the petals tightly in a glass container until there is one quart. Pour the boiling water over the petals and leave for 24 hours. Drain liquid from petals and add yeast and sugar to the liquid. Place in a stoneware crock for six weeks while the liquid ferments. Wine may then be strained and bottled. Be sure to use corks for bottling.

*Do not substitute another color.

Wassail

6 sticks cinnamon

16 cloves

1 teaspoon allspice

cheese cloth bag

3 medium oranges

6 cups apple juice

2 cups cranberry juice

¼ cup sugar

1 teaspoon bitters

1 cup rum (optional)

orange slices for garnish

Break up cinnamon sticks and tie with allspice in a cheese cloth bag. Stick oranges with cloves. In saucepan combine juices, sugar and bitters. Add bag of spices and oranges. Cover and simmer for 10 minutes. Stir in 1 cup of rum, if desired. Add slices of orange and serve warm.

Yield: 9 cups

Mr. Michie's Red Punch

2 quarts chilled apple cider

juice of one lemon

1 pint strawberries

fresh mint sprigs

1 quart Apple Jack brandy

2 cups sloe gin

2 bottles chilled champagne

Combine first six ingredients in punch bowl and stir. Pour chilled champagne on top. Mint and berries will float to top. Serve immediately.

Yield: 30 drinks

Michie Tavern's Red Punch Today

1 gallon chilled apple cider

juice of two lemons

1 cup puréed frozen strawberries

fresh mint sprigs

Combine ingredients in punch bowl. Mint and fruit will float to the top. Serve chilled.

Yield: 30 drinks

Soups

Golden Corn Chowder

4 cups diced potatoes

3 slices bacon, diced

2 medium onions, diced

2½ cups corn

¼ teaspoon celery salt

½ teaspoon pepper

½ teaspoon parsley flakes

6 cups milk

Cook the potatoes until tender. Sauté the bacon and onions in a frying pan, being sure not to overcook. Drain the potatoes. Drain the bacon and onions. Mix the potatoes, onions and bacon with the corn in a saucepan. Stir in the seasonings and the milk. Simmer over low heat for 20 to 25 minutes. Serve.

Yield: 8 servings

Asparagus Soup

3 tablespoons butter

1 small onion, minced

3 tablespoons flour

4 cups chicken stock

1 pound fresh asparagus

1 small potato, peeled and diced

Salt and freshly-ground pepper
   to taste

1 cup cream

Clean and cut asparagus into 1" pieces and reserve tips. Melt butter in saucepan and cook onion until soft. Whisk in flour until blended and gradually add chicken stock. Add asparagus pieces (not tips) and potato to stock and simmer 20 minutes. Add salt and freshly ground pepper to taste. Cool mixture slightly and puree in blender or food processor. Return to soup pot, stir in cream and warm through. In pot of boiling water, blanch asparagus tips until tender (1–2 minutes, time may vary). Drain well and garnish soup with tips.

Yield: 6 servings

Pea Soup

10 cups water

2 cups dry split green peas

1 ham bone

½ cup chopped onion

1 cup chopped celery

½ cup chopped carrot

1 clove garlic

1 bay leaf

1 teaspoon sugar

Dash of ground red pepper

Cut away any good chunks of ham from the ham bone and set them aside. Combine all ingredients in a large pot and bring to boil. Simmer, covered, for 3½ hours. Remove ham bone. Put soup through a sieve. Return to soup pot with ham chunks and simmer for 30 minutes longer.

Yield: 8 servings

Pumpkin Soup

5 cups pumpkin, boiled and mashed

2 medium onions, finely diced

5 tablespoons butter

2 cups chicken broth

4½ cups milk

¼ teaspoon cloves

¼ teaspoon ginger

¼ teaspoon allspice

¼ teaspoon cinnamon

1½ teaspoons sugar

¾ teaspoon salt

1 cup heavy cream

Strain the mashed pumpkin through a sieve into a dish.

In a 4-quart saucepan, sauté the onions in the butter until tender. Add the mashed pumpkin, broth, milk, spices, sugar and salt. Stir over medium-high heat until the soup boils. Reduce the heat and simmer gently, stirring continuously for 18 minutes. Pour the soup through a strainer. Return to low heat for approximately 5 minutes, adding the heavy cream; be sure not to boil the soup. Serve immediately.

Yield: 8 to 10 servings

 # Garden Vegetable Soup

2 tablespoons canola oil	15 ounces crushed tomatoes
2 cloves fresh garlic, diced	2 tablespoons tomato paste
1 diced onion	1 cup cut green beans
½ cup diced carrots	2 medium diced potatoes
½ cup diced green pepper	dash of ground red pepper
½ cup diced celery	freshly ground black pepper
6 cups chicken broth	1 cup shredded cabbage (optional)

Heat oil in large stock pot. Briefly sauté garlic then add onions, carrots, peppers, and celery. Cook until softened. Add broth, crushed tomatoes (with juice), and tomato paste and bring to boil. Add remaining ingredients (including cabbage, if desired). If there is not enough broth, add water until desired thickness. Return to boil. Turn down heat and simmer until all vegetables are soft.

Yield: 8 servings

Cheesy Chicken Chowder

4 tablespoons butter	2 cups diced cooked chicken
2 cups shredded carrots	1 cup corn, fresh or frozen
1/2 cup chopped onion	1 teaspoon Worcestershire sauce
1/2 cup flour	8 ounces shredded sharp
3 cups chicken broth	cheddar cheese
4 cups milk	salt, pepper to taste

Melt butter in a skillet. Add carrots and onion and saute until tender. Blend in flour. Then add broth and milk. Cook and stir until thick and smooth. Add remaining ingredients and stir until cheese is melted.

Yield: 8 servings

Peasant Soup

2 ounces extra virgin olive oil	4 large tomatoes, diced large
2 medium onions, diced	1 quart water, lightly flavored
2 zucchini, sliced	with chicken bouillon
2 large yellow squash, sliced	¼ teaspoon salt
2 large carrots, sliced	1 tablespoon sugar
2 red bell peppers, diced	¼ cup diced fresh herbs to
1 large butternut squash,	include: parsley, chives,
peeled and sliced	basil and thyme

Heat oil in soup pot. Start to sauté vegetables over medium heat, placing onion first and then the rest of the vegetables. When the juices start to extract from the vegetables, cover the pot and let them sweat over medium low heat. Stir frequently, cook until all vegetables are soft. Let cool a little and then puree in a food processor until smooth. Return to the stove, add water and seasonings, adjust to taste.

Yield: 12 servings

Creamed Potato Soup

9 medium potatoes, peeled
   and quartered
4 medium onions, diced
3 cups water
1 tablespoon parsley flakes

2 teaspoons celery salt
1 teaspoon black pepper
½ teaspoon salt
2 cups milk
2 tablespoons butter or margarine

Boil the potatoes and onions in the water until tender. Remove the potatoes and onions to mash. Add all of the spices to the broth; boil for 15 minutes. Return the mashed potatoes and onions to the broth, adding the milk and butter. Simmer over low heat for ½ hour; serve.

(**Note:** Additional milk may be used to attain desired consistency.)

Yield: 6 to 8 servings

Baked Potato Soup

5 to 6 large Irish potatoes
1 large onion, sliced
Salt, to taste
Black pepper, to taste
Garlic powder or garlic
   clove, to taste

½ pound grated cheddar cheese
1 quart milk
Chopped green onions, crumbled
   bacon, additional grated
   cheddar cheese

Peel and dice potatoes and onion. Boil in 5-quart pot with enough water to cover vegetables by an inch. Season with salt, pepper and garlic. Once the potatoes are well cooked and water has been reduced, mash the potatoes, but keep a few large chunks. Add grated cheese (adjust to your taste, you don't want your soup to be too yellow). Add milk slowly until you get the consistency you desire. Adjust seasonings to taste. Garnish with onions, bacon and cheese to taste.

Lentil Soup

1 pound lentil beans

3 to 3½ quarts water

1 ham bone

7 slices bacon, diced

3 large carrots, diced

3 medium onions, diced

3 stalks celery, thinly sliced

6- to 8-ounce can stewed tomatoes

1 tablespoon parsley flakes

½ teaspoon pepper

½ teaspoon thyme

¼ teaspoon garlic salt

Soak the lentils in water for 1½ hours; drain. Boil the water; add the ham bone and the lentils.

In a frying pan, sauté the bacon, carrots, onions and celery; add the sautéed mixture to the broth; cook until the soup thickens. Add the stewed tomatoes and seasonings. Allow the soup to simmer for 1 hour. Remove the ham bone. Serve.

Yield: 8 servings

Peanut Soup

2 medium onions, finely diced

2 stalks celery, finely diced

½ cup butter or margarine

2½ tablespoons all-purpose flour

8 cups chicken broth

2¾ cups peanut butter

3 cups light cream

¼ teaspoon salt

½ teaspoon celery salt

½ lemon

½ cup unsalted peanuts,
    finely chopped (optional)

In a large quart casserole dish, sauté the onions and celery in the butter until the vegetables are tender. Blend in the flour. Add the broth and boil rapidly, being sure to stir constantly to avoid scorching. Continue to boil until the broth thickens and becomes smooth. Cover and simmer for 18 minutes over low heat. Add the peanut butter and cream; blend thoroughly. Add the spices and juice from the lemon. Simmer for another 10 minutes over low heat. Add the peanuts. Stir and serve.

Yield: 8 servings

Turtle Soup

2 2½ pounds veal bones
2 quarts water or beef stock
2 chopped carrots
3 chopped celery ribs
1 chopped onion
6 ounces of tomato paste
Salt and pepper to taste
5 whole cloves
1 medium onion

2 tablespoons butter
1 tablespoon flour
1 medium-size can tomatoes, cut up
1 pound boiled fresh turtle meat
1 tablespoon parsley flakes
½ cup sherry
2 chopped boiled eggs
1 lemon, sliced

Combine veal bones, water or stock, carrots, celery, onion, tomato paste, salt, pepper and cloves and bring to a boil. Skim off scum that rises to the surface. Lower heat and simmer for two to three hours. Strain through cheesecloth and set broth aside. Sauté onion in butter and stir in flour until flour is light brown. Add canned tomatoes and cook about 15 minutes over medium heat. Combine with soup broth and add boiled turtle meat and parsley. Bring to a boil and remove from heat. Add ½ cup sherry and garnish with chopped boiled eggs and lemon slices.

Yield: 8 servings

Oyster Bisque

1 quart oysters	½ teaspoon salt
1 bay leaf	¼ teaspoon white pepper
2 medium chopped onions	1 pint light cream
2 ribs chopped celery	¼ cup dry sherry (optional)
½ cup butter	Fresh, chopped parsley (optional)
¼ cup all purpose flour	Paprika (optional)

Drain and chop oysters, reserve liquid. Add enough water to drained oyster liquid to make 2 quarts. Add bay leaf, 1 onion and 1 rib of celery and simmer uncovered for 30 minutes. Remove from heat and allow to "ripen" for at least 1 hour, then strain. Melt butter in saucepan and add remaining onion and celery. Sauté 5 minutes.

Stir in flour, but do not brown; remove from heat and add part of the oyster stock, stirring constantly. Return to heat and add remaining stock, stirring until smooth. Add salt and pepper. Cook over low heat for 10 minutes. Add oysters and cream; simmer gently for 2 or 3 minutes. If adding sherry, do so just before serving. Garnish with fresh chopped parsley or paprika for color.

Carrot Soup

2 pounds of carrots	1 tablespoon curry powder
1 large onion	8 ounces cream cheese
5 cups chicken broth	fresh ground pepper to taste

Peel carrots and chop into large pieces. Chop onion. Bring chicken broth to boil and add carrots, onion, and curry powder. Cover and cook over medium heat until vegetables are tender. Cool slightly and puree in blender with cream cheese. Add pepper to taste. Serve hot or cold.

Yield: 6 servings

Gazpacho

1 jalapeno pepper, diced
1 teaspoon Tabasco sauce
1 tablespoon fresh cilantro,
  finely chopped
1 tablespoon fresh parsley,
  finely chopped
3 large tomatoes, peeled,
  seeded and finely chopped

1 cucumber, peeled, seeded,
  and finely chopped
1 cup green, red or yellow pepper
2 tablespoons onion, chopped
2 tablespoons scallion, chopped
3 cups tomato juice
½ teaspoon red pepper
½ teaspoon cumin
½ teaspoon black pepper

Combine all ingredients and chill at least two hours. Add more freshly chopped parsley and cilantro if desired.

Yield: 6 servings

Potato, Broccoli, Cheese Chowder

2 tablespoons butter
1 pound Yukon Gold potatoes,
  peeled and chopped
1 large onion, chopped
1 teaspoon paprika
½ teaspoon dry mustard
1 cup water

2 cups milk
½ teaspoon salt
1½ cups chicken broth
1 cup fresh broccoli, chopped
1 cup corn
1½ cups shredded extra sharp
  cheddar cheese

Melt butter in large saucepot over medium heat. Add potatoes and onions and cook for about ten minutes until vegetables are tender. Stir in paprika and mustard and mix. Then add water, milk, salt, and pepper. Bring to a boil then reduce heat to low. Cover and simmer 15 minutes. Cool slightly then process soup in food processor or blender in two or three batches until smooth. Return to saucepot.. Add chicken broth, broccoli, and corn. Bring to boil again, and cook until vegetables are tender. Reduce heat, then stir in cheese gradually until melted. Serve immediately.

Breads

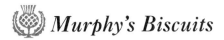 Murphy's Biscuits

2 cups all-purpose flour

2 teaspoons baking powder

¼ teaspoon salt

3 tablespoons shortening

⅔ cup whole milk

Sift together flour, baking powder and salt. Cut in shortening and then stir in milk quickly with fork to make dough light and fluffy but not sticky. Knead until dough is smooth, approximately 10 times. Roll out the dough on lightly floured board. Cut into biscuits ½-inch thick. Bake on greased cookie sheet at 450° for 8 to 10 minutes.

Yield: 10 to 12 biscuits

Rolled Cheese Biscuits

3 cups self-rising flour

½ cup shortening

1½ cups grated sharp
   cheddar cheese

1 cup plus 2 tablespoons
   buttermilk

¼ teaspoon baking soda

Combine flour and shortening in a medium bowl; cut in shortening with pastry blender until mixture resembles coarse meal. Stir in cheese.

Combine buttermilk and soda; pour into flour mixture and stir well. Turn dough out onto a lightly floured surface, and knead lightly 3 or 4 times.

Roll dough to 3/4-inch thickness; cut into rounds with a 1½-inch cutter. Place biscuits on lightly greased baking sheets; bake at 450° for 10 to 12 minutes.

Yield: 3 dozen.

Drop Cheese Biscuits

1 cup flour	2 cups sharp cheddar cheese, grated
1½ teaspoons baking powder	½ cup milk
½ teaspoon salt	2 tablespoons cold butter

Sift flour, baking powder, and salt in a bowl. Cut in the butter with a pastry cutter until mixture resembles coarse meal. Stir in the cheddar and add enough milk to make a soft, sticky dough. Drop by rounded tablespoons onto greased baking sheet. Bake at 425° for 15 minutes.

Yield: 16 biscuits

Sweet Potato Biscuits

1½ cups flour	4 tablespoons sugar
4 teaspoons baking powder	4 tablespoons shortening
½ teaspoon salt	1¼ cups mashed sweet potatoes

Sift together flour, baking powder, salt. Add sugar and shortening to sweet potatoes. Combine potato and flour mixture. Knead and fold out to ½-inch thick. Bake at 425° for 12 to 15 minutes or until done.

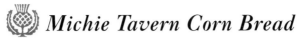

Michie Tavern Corn Bread
FROM THE ORDINARY

2 cups self-rising white stone ground corn meal

½ cup sugar

¾ cup milk

2 eggs

½ cup canola oil

Sift together corn meal and sugar in a large bowl. Add milk, eggs and oil. Stir with a wooden spoon just until all ingredients are wet and smooth. Bake in a greased 8-inch square pan in preheated oven at 425° for 15–20 minutes. Cut into squares and serve. Note: To achieve Michie Tavern's same consistency and crunchiness, use the exact corn meal suggested here.

Yield: 9 to 12 servings

Crackling Skillet Bread

1 cup all-purpose flour

2 cups cornmeal

3 tablespoons sugar

3 tablespoons baking powder

1½ teaspoons salt

1 teaspoon soda

2 eggs, well beaten

1 cup buttermilk

¼ cup bacon drippings

1 cup cracklings or ½ pound bacon

Heat oven to 375°. Grease skillet or use reserve drippings from bacon. Combine flour, cornmeal, sugar, baking powder, salt and soda; combine eggs, buttermilk and ¼ cup drippings. Add liquid ingredients to dry ingredients all at once; add cracklings or crumbled bacon. Beat well; pour into skillet. Bake for 25 minutes or until golden brown. Serve while hot.

Yield: 8 to 10 slices

Cornmeal Puffs

1 yeast cake

¼ cup lukewarm water

1 cup milk

½ cup shortening or oil

¼ cup sugar

1 cup self-rising cornmeal

3 cups self-rising flour

2 eggs

Dissolve yeast in lukewarm water. Heat milk and pour into bowl containing shortening and sugar. Stir to dissolve and then cool. Stir in cornmeal and 1 cup flour. Beat until smooth. Beat in yeast and eggs. Stir in enough flour to make a stiff batter. Beat until smooth and elastic. Cover and let rise in warm place until light and bubbly (about one hour). Stir down and fill greased muffin cups half full. Sprinkle lightly with meal. Let rise in warm place until doubled, about 30 minutes. Bake at 400° for 15 to 20 minutes.

Yield: 2 dozen

Cornmeal Batter Cakes

1 cup flour

1 cup white cornmeal

2 teaspoons baking powder

1 teaspoon salt

½ teaspoon baking soda

2 cups buttermilk

½ cup water if needed

2 eggs, well beaten

Sift dry ingredients. Combine buttermilk, water and eggs. Add to dry ingredients. Stir until smooth. Add more water if necessary as batter must be thin. Pour 1 teaspoon of the mixture on to a hot greased griddle. When bubbles form, turn and brown. Serve with syrup or honey.

Yield: 10 to 12 cakes

Hush Puppies

2 cups cornmeal, white or yellow
1 tablespoon flour
1 teaspoon baking powder
½ teaspoon soda

1 teaspoon salt
1 clove minced garlic
1 cup buttermilk
1 beaten egg

Combine dry ingredients; add garlic, buttermilk and egg. Mix well. Fry tablespoons of batter in deep hot fat (about 370°) until golden brown. Drain on paper towels. Serve hot.

You may use less milk to make a stiff batter that can be shaped into small cakes. Fry as above. Add sage and some whole grain corn, if desired.

Yield: 30 hush puppies

The Real Corn Pone

2 cups white corn meal
3 cups boiling water

1 teaspoon salt
1 tablespoon butter

Scald corn meal with boiling water; add salt and butter. Mixture will be very stiff. Make a pone, pat in one hand and place in well greased heavy pan. Bake at 400° about 30 minutes. Put under broiler to brown.

Yield: 6 to 8 servings

Old-Fashioned Spoon Bread

½ cup boiling water

¼ teaspoon salt

1 cup cornmeal

2½ cups milk

3 tablespoons butter

2 eggs, well-beaten

1½ teaspoons baking powder

Preheat oven to 350°. Butter a medium-sized baking dish. Mix together the boiling water, salt and cornmeal. Simmer the milk until hot. Add the milk and butter to the mix. Let stand for 15 minutes. Beat in the eggs, one at a time, adding the baking powder. Pour the batter into the baking dish. Bake for 30 to 40 minutes. Serve hot with butter.

Yield: 4 to 6 servings

Note: For a sweet spoon bread, substitute 1 teaspoon sugar for the salt.

Sally Lunn

1 cup milk

1 yeast cake

½ cup margarine or butter

5½ tablespoons sugar

3 beaten eggs

1 teaspoon salt

4 cups all-purpose flour

Simmer the milk over low heat, but do not boil. Add the yeast cake. Cream the butter and sugar; blend in the eggs. Sift together the salt and flour. Blend the three mixes together. Set aside the batter, allowing the mix to rise until doubled in bulk; beat again thoroughly. Empty the batter into a greased tube cake pan. Let rise to double again. Bake at 325° for 1 hour.

Notes on Kneading Bread

1. When enough flour has been mixed in, the dough is soft and biscuit-like and stretchy when pulled. Turn it out onto a floured surface and it is ready for kneading.

2. First, knead the edge of the dough farthest from you and then fold in toward the center.

3. With heels of hands press edge of dough down into center and push away from you, giving the dough a quarter turn. Repeat over and over with a strong, steady rhythm.

4. When you have kneaded enough, turn over the now smooth, silky dough so that creases are underneath. Shape into a ball. Put in bowl. Cover and let rise in a warm place.

Yeast Rolls

¾ cup sugar

2½ cups warm water

3 packages yeast

½ cup oil

1 tablespoon salt

2 quarts flour

¾ cup powdered milk

Dissolve sugar in water. Sprinkle yeast over mixture. Let stand a few minutes. Add oil and salt. Stir. Add dry ingredients. Work with hands until soft dough forms. Grease with oil the sides and bottom of large bowl. Put dough into bowl and grease top. Let rise 45 minutes. Punch down, roll out and cut rolls with biscuit cutter. Place on greased cookie sheet. Let rise 45 minutes. Brush tops with melted butter. Bake at 400° for 10 minutes or until golden brown.

Yield: 5 dozen

Easy Yeast Bread

½ cup lukewarm water

1 package active dry yeast

1 cup milk

1 cup buttermilk or yogurt

3 tablespoons honey

2 cups whole wheat flour

3¼ cups of unbleached white flour

2 tablespoons vegetable oil

1 teaspoon salt

1 teaspoon baking soda

1 teaspoon baking powder

Cornmeal for dusting the pan

Dissolve yeast in lukewarm water for 5 minutes. Heat milk and buttermilk in small saucepan to just about body temperature. Transfer to mixing bowl. Stir in dissolved yeast and honey. Mix in whole wheat flour until smooth. Set aside. Cover, in a draft free area for 15 minutes or until bubbly. Stir oil into mixture. In a separate bowl mix 2 cups white flour with salt, baking soda and baking powder. Stir into yeast mixture, 1 cup at a time. Preheat oven to 425°. Turn dough onto a floured surface, knead for five minutes using remaining flour. Be gentle with this soft dough, but do not pamper it. Divide into two footballs. Dust pan with cornmeal and place loaves on baking sheet with room for expansion. Dust pan with cornmeal. Let loaves sit for 10 minutes in a warm, draft free area. Bake at 425° for 30 minutes or until loaves are well browned on all sides and bottoms make a hollow sound when tapped. Let cool for 30 minutes.

Yield: 2 loaves

Colonial Bread

¼ ounce dry yeast

1½ teaspoons salt

2½ tablespoons sugar

4 cups unbleached flour, sifted

¼ cup butter

1 cup warm water

1 egg

Combine the dry yeast, salt and sugar with 1 cup flour in a large bowl; mix thoroughly. Melt the butter in water over low heat until the liquid is quite warm. Combine the two mixtures. With a mixer, blend for 2 minutes at medium speed. Add enough flour to make the batter thick. Add the egg; beat at high speed for 2 minutes. Blend in 1½ cups flour to make the dough soft.

On a lightly floured board, knead the dough for 10 minutes; add flour as needed. Place the dough into a greased bowl, being sure to turn the dough so that the top and sides are also greased. Cover with a damp kitchen towel and set in a warm, dry place for 1½ hours. Let the dough rise until doubled in bulk.

Grease a loaf pan. Return the dough to the board. Knead the dough flat and cover with the towel. Let the dough stand for 20 minutes.

Roll the dough out and re-roll, jelly-roll style. Punch down the ends to seal. Turn the ends under and place the dough into the loaf pan. Cover the pan with the damp towel; set the pan in a warm, dry place for 1 hour or until the dough rises again. Bake at 350° for 45 minutes or until the crust is golden brown. Remove from the pan. Slice and serve immediately with butter. Or, allow the bread to cool.

Yield: 1 loaf

Cinnamon Sweet Rolls

1 cup milk
1 cup water
½ cup butter or margarine
6 to 6½ cups all-purpose flour,
    divided
½ cup sugar
3 packages dry yeast
1 teaspoon salt
1 egg, beaten

2 tablespoons butter or margarine,
    melted
⅓ cup firmly packed brown sugar
1½ teaspoons ground cinnamon
½ cup raisins
½ cup pecans, chopped
1 cup sifted powdered sugar
2 tablespoons milk
½ teaspoon vanilla extract

Combine first 3 ingredients in a small saucepan; heat until very warm (120°). Combine 2 cups flour and next 3 ingredients in a large bowl; stir well. Gradually add milk mixture to flour mixture, stirring well; add egg. Beat at medium speed of an electric mixer until smooth. Gradually stir in enough remaining flour to make a slightly stiff dough.

Turn dough out onto a well-floured surface, and knead until smooth and elastic (10 minutes). Place in a greased bowl, turning to grease top. Cover and let rise in a warm place (85°), free from drafts, one hour or until doubled in bulk.

Punch dough down, cover, and let rest 15 minutes. Set half of dough aside.

Turn remaining half of dough out onto a lightly floured surface; roll to a 20- x 12-inch rectangle; brush 2 tablespoons butter over dough, leaving a ½-inch border. Combine brown sugar, cinnamon, raisins and pecans; sprinkle mixture over rectangle. Beginning at long side, roll up jellyroll style; press edges and ends together securely. Cut into 1-inch slices; place cut side down on a greased cookie sheet. Cover with greased plastic wrap; refrigerate 8 hours. Repeat with remaining dough.

Before baking, leave covered and let rise in a warm place (85°), free from drafts, one hour or until doubled in bulk. Bake at 375° for 20 minutes.

Combine powdered sugar, milk, and vanilla; drizzle over warm rolls.

Yield: 40 rolls

Lazy Sweet Bread

2 yeast cakes, dissolved in
  ¼ cup hot water
¼ cup butter or margarine
½ cup sugar

1 cup whole milk
2 eggs, well-beaten
4½ cups all-purpose flour, sifted
1 teaspoon salt

Dissolve the yeast in ¼ cup boiling water. Add the yeast to the butter, sugar, salt and milk. Mix with the eggs and flour. When the dough has been well-mixed, place on a floured board and knead until shiny in appearance. Place the dough into a greased bowl; cover with a damp kitchen towel. Let the dough rise until doubled in bulk. Knead the dough again and shape for a loaf pan. Place the dough in the greased loaf pan; cover with the towel and let rise again. Bake at 375° for 45 to 50 minutes.

Yield: 1 loaf

Maureen's Soda Bread

2 cups unsifted all-purpose flour
2 tablespoons sugar
2 teaspoons baking powder
1 teaspoon baking soda
½ teaspoon salt

3 tablespoons butter or
  margarine, softened
1 cup buttermilk
1 tablespoons butter or
  margarine, melted

Lightly grease a small cookie sheet. Combine dry ingredients and then cut in softened butter with a pastry blender or fork until mixture looks like fine crumbs. Add buttermilk; mix in with a fork only until dry ingredients are moistened. Turn out on lightly floured pastry cloth or board. Knead gently until smooth—about 1 minute. Shape into a ball. Place on prepared cookie sheet; flatten into a 7-inch circle. (Dough will be about 1½ inches thick). Press a large floured knife into center of loaf almost through to bottom. Repeat at right angle, to divide loaf into quarters. Bake at 375° for 30 to 40 minutes or until top is golden and loaf sounds hollow when tapped. Remove to wire rack to cool. Brush top with melted butter. Dust with flour, if you wish.

Yield: 1 loaf

Coffee Cake

½ cup shortening

¾ cups white sugar

1 teaspoon vanilla extract

3 eggs

2 cups sifted flour

1 teaspoon baking soda

1 teaspoon baking powder

1 cup sour cream

6 tablespoons butter or margarine

1 cup firmly packed, softened
  brown sugar

2 teaspoons cinnamon

1 cup chopped nuts

Cream shortening, white sugar and vanilla thoroughly. Add eggs one at a time, beating after each addition. Sift flour, baking soda, and baking powder. Add to creamed mixture alternately with sour cream, blending after each addition. Spread half of batter in 10-inch tube pan that has been greased and lined on bottom with waxed paper.

Cream butter, brown sugar and cinnamon together. Add nuts, mix well. Dot batter in pan evenly with half of nut mixture. Cover with remaining batter. Dot top with remaining nut mixture. Bake at 350° about 50 minutes. Cool cake 10 minutes, remove from pan.

Yield: 10–12 servings

Whole Wheat Soda Bread

1 cup all-purpose flour

1 teaspoon baking powder

1 teaspoon baking soda

½ teaspoon salt

2 cups whole wheat flour

1½ cups buttermilk

1 tablespoon butter or margarine, melted

Preheat oven to 375°. Grease well a small cookie sheet. Into large mixing bowl, sift together all-purpose flour, baking powder, soda and salt. Add whole wheat flour; mix well with a fork. Add buttermilk; mix just until dry ingredients are moistened. Turn out on lightly floured pastry cloth or board. Knead gently until smooth—about 1 minute. Shape dough into a ball. Place on prepared cookie sheet; flatten into a 7-inch circle. (Dough will be about 1½ inches thick). Press a large floured knife into center of loaf almost through to bottom. Repeat, at right angle, to divide the loaf into quarters. Bake 40 minutes, or until top is golden and loaf sounds hollow when tapped. Remove to wire rack. Brush top with melted butter. Cool completely.

Yield: 1 loaf.

Irish Hot Bread

2 cups flour

4 teaspoons baking powder

½ teaspoon salt

1 tablespoon sugar

¾ cup seedless raisins

1 tablespoon caraway seeds

¾ cup milk

Sift flour, baking powder, salt and sugar. Mix in raisins and caraway seeds. Add milk; mix to form a soft dough. Turn onto a lightly floured surface. Shape gently into a flat, round loaf. Place in a greased deep 8-inch iron skillet or layer pan. Pat to fit pan. Brush top with milk. Bake at 400° for 5 minutes. Reduce to 350° and bake about 30 minutes.

Yield: 8-inch loaf

Countryside Garlic Herb Bread

6 teaspoons vegetable oil

7 teaspoons sugar

1 cup cold water

3 teaspoons celery salt

1 cup boiling water

1 bay leaf

1 packet yeast

4 teaspoons chives

½ teaspoon basil

¼ teaspoon thyme

¼ teaspoon sage

¼ teaspoon rosemary

2 teaspoons parsley flakes

6 cups all-purpose flour, sifted

½ cup butter, melted

2 tablespoons garlic salt (add more or less as desired)

Combine the oil, sugar, cold water and celery salt in a large bowl. In 1 cup boiling water, drop the bay leaf. Cover and boil the leaf for 5 minutes. Discard the leaf; pour the water into a measuring cup. Add enough hot water to equal 1 cup. Drop the yeast into the water, stirring to dissolve. Add the dissolved yeast to the other mixture. Stir in the spices, excluding the garlic salt. Gradually blend in the flour. Knead for 5 minutes. Place the dough into a buttered bowl and cover with a damp kitchen towel. Let stand in a warm, dry place for 90 minutes or until the dough is doubled in bulk. Knead down; let the dough stand for another 20 minutes. Evenly separate the dough, shaping each as desired: as a round loaf or as a loaf with tapered ends. Place the loaves on greased cookies sheets. Cover with the towel and let stand for 75 minutes or until the dough has doubled again. Bake at 350° for approximately 40 to 50 minutes or until brown.

Allow the bread to cool for 15 minutes on a rack. Slice each loaf. Blend the melted butter and garlic salt. Brush the garlic-butter mixture on sides of each slice. Serve immediately.

Yield: 2 loaves (approximately 18 servings)

Irish Scones

2 cups sifted flour

1 teaspoon salt

½ teaspoon baking soda

¼ cup butter or margarine

1 cup thick buttermilk or sour milk

Sift together dry ingredients. Cut in butter, finely. Add buttermilk gradually to form a stiff dough. Turn out on lightly floured surface. Knead about 10 times. Shape into a ball. Roll out into an 8-inch circle. Cut into 12 triangles or squares. Brush with milk. Bake at 400° for 15 to 20 minutes.

Yield: 12 scones

Banana Date Scones

2 cups flour

1 tablespoon sugar

2½ teaspoons baking powder

1 teaspoon salt

¼ cup butter

2 eggs

¼ cup whipping cream

2 ripe medium bananas, mashed

¾ cup chopped dates

In a mixing bowl, stir together flour, sugar, baking powder and salt. Cut in butter until mixture is crumbly. Beat eggs; reserve 2 tablespoons egg mixture. To remaining egg, add cream and bananas. Add banana mixture all at once to flour mixture, along with dates; stir gently until moistened. Turn onto lightly floured board. Pat out gently with floured hands to ½-inch thick. Cut into diamond shapes and place on lightly greased baking sheets. Brush top with reserved egg and sprinkle with sugar. Bake in 450° oven for 15 minutes. Serve warm.

Yield: 1 dozen

Pumpkin Bread

3 cups sugar

½ teaspoon baking powder

2 teaspoons baking soda

1½ teaspoons salt

1 teaspoon cinnamon

1 teaspoon nutmeg

1 teaspoon clove

3⅓ cups flour

1 cup oil

1 cup water

2 cups canned pumpkin

4 eggs

In a small bowl, beat eggs. In large bowl, combine all ingredients, including beaten eggs. Pour batter into two greased loaf pans. Bake at 325° for 90 minutes or until toothpick comes out clean.

Yield: 2 loaves

Oatmeal-Honey Loaf

1 cup steel-cut Irish oatmeal

1 cup boiling water

2¼ cup unsifted all-purpose flour

2½ teaspoons baking powder

1 teaspoon salt

¼ cup butter or margarine

3 tablespoons honey

1 egg

⅔ cup milk

In a large bowl, combine oatmeal and boiling water; stir until well mixed. Let stand until cool—about 2 hours. Lightly grease a 9 x 5 x 3-inch loaf pan. In medium bowl, sift together flour, baking powder and salt. Add butter and honey to oatmeal; mix well with wooden spoon. In small bowl, beat egg with the milk. To oatmeal mixture add flour mixture, then egg and milk; mix just until combined. Do not over mix. Turn into prepared pan. Bake at 350° for 70 minutes, or until crust is golden and toothpick inserted in center comes out clean. Turn out of pan onto cooling rack. Let cool completely before slicing into thin slices.

Yield: 1 loaf

Blueberry Banana Bread

1 cup fresh blueberries

1¾ cups all-purpose flour, divided

2 teaspoons baking powder

¼ teaspoon baking soda

¼ teaspoon salt

¼ teaspoon ground nutmeg

¼ cup unsalted butter, softened

¼ cup plus 2 tablespoons sugar

2 eggs

1 cup mashed ripe banana

Toss blueberries with 2 tablespoons flour, and set aside. Combine remaining flour, baking powder, soda, salt, and nutmeg in small bowl. Cream butter in a large bowl; gradually add sugar, beating at medium speed of electric mixer. Add eggs, one at a time, beating well after each addition. Add flour mixture alternately with mashed banana, beginning and ending with flour mixture. Mix just until dry ingredients are moistened. Gently fold in reserved blueberries.

Spoon batter into 8½ x 4½ x 3-inch greased loaf pan. Bake at 350° for 45 minutes or until a toothpick inserted in center comes out clean. Let cool in pan 10 minutes; remove to wire rack and cool completely.

Yield: 1 loaf

Zucchini Bread

3 cups peeled, grated zucchini

1⅔ cup sugar

⅔ cup vegetable oil

2 teaspoons vanilla

4 large eggs

3 cups all-purpose flour

1 teaspoon salt

2 teaspoons baking soda

1 teaspoon cinnamon

½ teaspoon baking powder

½ cup raisins

½ cup nut pieces

Grease bottom only of 9 x 5 x 3-inch loaf pan. Mix zucchini, sugar, oil, vanilla and eggs in large bowl. Stir in remaining ingredients. Pour into pans. Bake at 350° for 1 hour and 10 to 20 minutes, until toothpick inserted in center comes out clean. Cool on wire rack.

Yield: 2 loaves

Popovers

1 cup milk

1 tablespoon melted butter

1 cup all-purpose flour

¼ teaspoon salt

2 eggs

Beat milk, melted butter, flour, and salt until smooth. Mix in one egg at a time, but do not overbeat. Batter should be no heavier than whipping cream. Grease and flour deep muffin or popover pans, and fill them no more than ¾ full. Bake immediately in a pre-heated 450° oven. After 15 minutes, lower heat to 350°. Do not open the oven. Continue to bake for 20 more minutes. Test one popover for doneness by removing it and checking to see if the sidewalls are firm. If popovers are not cooked long enough, they will collapse.

Yield: 6 to 8 popovers

Bran Muffins

2 cups whole-grain flour

1½ cups bran

2 tablespoons sugar

¼ teaspoon salt

1¼ teaspoon baking soda

2 teaspoons cinnamon

2 cups buttermilk

2 egg whites

¼ cup honey

4 tablespoons melted butter

½ cup pecan pieces

½ cup raisins

Combine dry ingredients. Beat buttermilk, egg whites, honey, and butter. Blend the dry and liquid ingredients with a few swift strokes. Fold in, before the dry ingredients are entirely moist, pecan pieces and raisins. Pour into greased muffin tins. Bake at 350° for 20 minutes.

Yield: approximately 2 dozen

Cranberry Muffins

½ cup brown sugar

2 eggs, well-beaten

½ cup butter

2 teaspoons orange extract

1¾ cups all-purpose flour

2 tablespoons baking powder

1 teaspoon salt

½ teaspoon nutmeg

2 cups raw cranberries, finely chopped

½ cup raisins, finely chopped

Cream together the sugar, eggs, butter and extract. Sift together the flour, powder, salt and nutmeg. Combine the two mixtures to make a thick dough. Use milk to moisten the dough if necessary. Stir in the chopped cranberries and raisins. Bake at 350° for 12 to 15 minutes in greased muffin tins.

Yield: approximately 2 dozen

Sweet Potato Muffins

½ cup butter or margarine, softened

1¼ cups sugar

2 eggs

1¼ cups mashed sweet potatoes

¼ to ⅓ cup milk

1½ cups all-purpose flour

2 teaspoons baking powder

¼ teaspoon salt

1 teaspoon ground cinnamon

1 teaspoon ground nutmeg

Cream butter; gradually add 1¼ cups sugar, beating at medium speed of an electric mixer. Add eggs, one at a time, beating well after each addition. Stir in sweet potatoes and milk. Combine flour, baking powder, salt, cinnamon and nutmeg; add to creamed mixture, stirring just until moistened. Spoon into greased muffin pans, filling two-thirds full. Bake at 400° for 20 to 25 minutes.

Yield: 1 dozen

Old Dominion Cinnamon Raisin Bread

2 yeast cakes, dissolved in ¼ cup hot water

¼ cup butter or margarine

6 tablespoons brown sugar

1 teaspoon salt

1 cup whole milk

2 eggs, well-beaten

4½ cups flour

1 cup raisins

6 tablespoons sugar

6 tablespoons cinnamon

Combine the following ingredients in a large mixing bowl: the dissolved yeast, butter or margarine, brown sugar, salt and milk. Beat in the eggs, flour and raisins. When the dough is well-mixed, place on a floured board and knead until satiny in appearance. Place the dough into a greased bowl and cover with a damp kitchen towel. Let the dough rise until doubled in bulk. Knead the dough again and roll out. Mix the cinnamon and sugar together. Sprinkle ⅔ of the sugar-cinnamon mix over the rolled out dough. Roll the dough back up, jelly-roll style. Place the dough in a greased loaf pan; let rise a second time. Place a few pats of butter on top and garnish with the remaining sugar-cinnamon mix. Bake at 375° for 55 to 60 minutes. Allow a few minutes to cool. Serve with apple butter or let the bread cool completely and wrap in a plastic bag and store in the refrigerator for later use.

Yield: 1 loaf

Vegetables

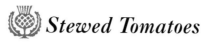 # *Stewed Tomatoes*

4 cups whole tomatoes,
   peeled and quartered
½ cup sugar

¼ stick butter, melted
½ teaspoon salt
6 baked biscuits

Mix together the tomatoes, sugar, butter and salt. Crumble the biscuits and add to the mixture. Cover and cook in saucepan over medium heat for 15 minutes.

Yield: 6 servings

Stewed Tomatoes and Corn

4 cups peeled, quartered
   ripe tomatoes
2 cups fresh corn cut from the cob
3 tablespoons butter

½ teaspoon salt
Freshly-ground pepper to taste
1 teaspoon sugar

Melt butter in saucepan. Add tomatoes and corn and simmer until vegetables are tender. Stir often to prevent vegetables from sticking to pan. Add salt, pepper and sugar. Simmer over low heat for about 15 minutes. Serve hot.

Yield: 6 servings

Fried Green Tomatoes

1 egg

½ cup milk

¼ cup all-purpose flour

½ cup cornmeal

4 large, firm green tomatoes,
    cut in ⅛- to ¼-inch slices

Vegetable shortening for frying

Beat egg and milk together. In separate bowl, combine flour and cornmeal.
Dip each tomato slice in egg liquid, then in dry ingredients. Melt shortening
to measure ½-inch depth in heavy skillet. Place tomato slices carefully in hot
shortening and fry, turning once, until brown on both sides. Drain on paper
towels. Season with salt.

Yields: 4 to 6 servings

Yuletide Yams

40-ounce can sliced yams,
    reserve liquid

¼ cup brown sugar

1 tablespoon sugar

½ teaspoon cinnamon

¼ teaspoon nutmeg

1 teaspoon cornstarch

1 teaspoon water

½ cup chopped pecans

mini marshmallows

Drain yams and reserve one cup of liquid. Spread yams in 10" by 6" pan.
In small saucepan, heat 3/4 cup reserved liquid from yams and gradually add
sugars and spices. Mix cornstarch and cold water in small bowl. As liquid
heats, add one teaspoon of cornstarch mixture to thicken sauce. Add another
teaspoon if needed or thin with remaining 1/4 cup liquid if necessary.
Sauce should resemble thick syrup. Remove sauce from heat and stir in
pecans. Ladle over yams. Bake uncovered for 20 minutes at 350° or until
warmed through. Remove from stove and sprinkle with single layer of mini
marshmallows (about two cups). Return to oven until marshmallows are
browned. Do not overcook. Note: Recipe doubles well.

Yield: 6 to 8 servings

Mashed Parsnips

2 pounds parsnips, peeled
 and sliced
4 tablespoons butter

1 teaspoon salt
1¼ cups cream

Place parsnips in pot and cover with water. Boil until tender, about 25 minutes, and drain. Mash gently and add butter until melted. Gradually add cream. If needed, add a little flour to thicken. Stir in salt, and add pepper if desired.

Yield: 6 servings

Broccoli Mousse

Mousse:

2 pounds broccoli
¼ cup whipping cream
1 egg

salt, pepper to taste
pinch of nutmeg

Sauce:

1 tablespoon lemon juice
1 tablespoon whipping cream

½ cup butter

Cut up broccoli and steam until tender. Drain all liquid then puree. Add whipping cream, egg and spices. Grease muffin tins. Put tins in tray of water and bake at 350° for 45 minutes. Cool. To make sauce, melt butter in saucepan over low heat. Stir in whipping cream and lemon juice. Stir until warm and slightly thickened. Turn out mousse from muffin tins and spoon sauce over mousse.

Yield: 4–6 servings

Lamplighter's Squash Casserole

1 pound zucchini squash,
    thinly sliced
1 pound summer (yellow)
    squash, thinly sliced
½ pound ground beef
1 tablespoon parsley flakes
1 tablespoon oregano flakes
1 teaspoon pepper
½ teaspoon salt
¼ teaspoon garlic salt

2 medium onions, diced
2 medium peppers, diced
¾ cup mushrooms, sliced
6 ounces tomato paste
12 ounces tomato sauce
12 ounces mozzarella cheese,
    shredded or grated
½ cup cracker or bread crumbs
½ cup Parmesan cheese, grated

Boil squash in 1 cup of water until tender. Brown ground beef with spices, onions, peppers and mushrooms. When the onions are tender, add tomato paste and sauce; stir. Cover and simmer over low heat for 30 to 40 minutes. Drain squash. In a baking dish spread a layer of sauce; cover with a layer of squash, then ½ of the mozzarella cheese. Repeat. Cover the top with the remaining sauce. Mix the bread crumbs with the Parmesan cheese and sprinkle the mix over the top of the casserole. Bake at 325° for 20 minutes.

Yield: 8 servings

Yuletide Squash Casserole

4–6 medium yellow squash
4 tablespoons butter, divided

½ medium onion, sliced
1 cup white bread crumbs

Wash and slice squash into 1/4" rounds. Steam squash just until tender and drain. Julienne onion into long, thin slices. Melt 2 tablespoons butter in saucepan and sauté onions until translucent. Butter the bottom of a 2-quart round casserole or 9"-square pan. Line bottom of dish with half of bread crumbs. Layer squash and onions on bread crumbs then sprinkle remaining bread crumbs on top of vegetables. Melt remaining butter and pour over crumbs. Bake at 300° for 30 minutes.

Yield: 6 servings

Baked Stuffed Squash

2 medium acorn squash	Dash of nutmeg
Salt and pepper to taste	6 tablespoons cream
8 tablespoons butter	2 tablespoons brown sugar
Dash cloves	¼ cup maple syrup

Cut the squash into halves; clean out the seeds and discard. Sprinkle the squash with salt and pepper; add 1 tablespoon butter to each half. Bake, open-side up in a casserole dish at 350° for 6 minutes or until the squash is tender.

Scrape out the squash into a bowl, being careful not to break the shell. Add the cloves, nutmeg and cream to the squash. Blend well. Fill the shells with the squash mixture. Cream together the remaining butter and sugar. Divide the creamed mixture evenly, placing on top of the squash in each shell. Pour a little maple syrup over the top of each. Bake at 325° for 20 to 30 minutes or until the squash turns golden brown.

Yield: 4 servings

Southern Squash Casserole

4 medium yellow squash, sliced	Salt & pepper to taste
1 medium onion, sliced	½ cup sharp cheddar cheese, grated
2 eggs	½ cup cracker or bread crumbs
½ cup milk	1 tablespoon butter or margarine

Steam squash and onions until tender, about 5 minutes. In small bowl beat eggs with milk, salt and pepper. Lightly grease casserole pan and spoon in steamed squash and onions. Pour egg mixture over vegetables. Top with cheese, crumbs and dot with butter. Bake at 350° from 30 to 40 minutes until firm.

Yield: 6 servings

Mashed Turnips

3 small yellow turnips

¼ cup butter

1 tablespoon sugar (optional)

2 teaspoons salt

2 teaspoons pepper

Dash of cloves

Dash of nutmeg

Dash of thyme

¼ cup heavy cream

In a large pot filled with salted water, cook the turnips for 22 minutes or until tender; drain and mash. Add the butter and seasonings; mix well. Add the cream, stirring until smooth.

Yield: 6 servings

Mrs. Michie's Southern Beets

FROM THE ORDINARY

1 pound fresh beets

¼ cup sugar

¼ cup vinegar

3 tablespoons water

¾ of a small onion (diced)

Salt and pepper to taste

Boil beets approximately one hour (depending on size), skin, slice and set aside. (If canned beets are used, include juices and eliminate water.) Combine sugar, vinegar and water; then add beets, diced onion, salt and pepper. Cover and marinate in refrigerator about eight hours.

Yield: 4 to 6 servings

Marinated Green Bean Salad

1-pound can green beans
   that are cut and firm
½ cup vinegar
½ cup salad oil

2 tablespoons sugar
2 teaspoons garlic salt
1½ teaspoon ground oregano
1 teaspoon pepper

Drain beans and set aside. In a large bowl combine all other ingredients and whisk well. Add the beans, gently stir and chill for one hour. Before serving, stir to distribute marinade.

Yield: 4 to 6 servings

"Yeller" Bean Salad

1 cup cooked green or wax
   (yellow) beans, cut French-style
1 cup cooked peas
1 cup cooked corn

1 medium onion, chopped
4 ounces pimentos, diced
1½ cups vegetable oil
¾ cup vinegar

Drain the canned vegetables. Combine all of the ingredients in a large bowl. Cover and marinate in refrigerator for 24 hours. Mix again before serving.

Yield: 6 to 8 servings

Fiddler's Three Bean Salad

1 pound can cut green beans, drained

1 pound can cut wax beans, drained

1 pound can kidney beans, drained

1 cup vinegar

1 cup oil

1 tablespoon sugar

3 teaspoons oregano flakes

3 teaspoons garlic salt

1 tablespoon pepper

2 whole sweet pimentos,
   finely chopped

Mix all of the ingredients together. Marinate covered in refrigerator for 12 hours. Mix again before serving.

Yield: 4 to 6 servings

Lentil and Vegetable Medley

2½ cups lentils

3 cloves garlic

1 medium onion

2 medium carrots

butter or oil for cooking

1 12- to 16-ounce can plum tomatoes

6 ounces tomato paste

1 quart water

Salt and pepper to taste

Wash lentils. Place in soup pot with enough water to cover by 2" and boil for 20 minutes. Drain lentils and set aside. Peel and dice garlic, onions and carrots. Using soup pot, sauté vegetables in butter or oil until onions are translucent, approximately 7 to 8 minutes. Add lentils and continue to sauté for another minute or two. Add plum tomatoes with juice, tomato paste, one quart of water and cook for 35 minutes. Add salt and pepper to taste. Serve as is or over brown rice and sprinkle with Parmesan cheese.

Yield: 10 to 12 servings

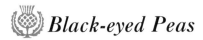 Black-eyed Peas

1 pound fresh black-eyed peas	½ teaspoon garlic salt
1 ham hock or 1 slice salt pork	1 teaspoon pepper
1 teaspoon seasoning salt	1 tablespoon butter

Rinse the peas thoroughly; strain. In a large pot, add the peas and pork with enough water to cover. Cook for 50 minutes or until the peas are tender. Gently mix in the pepper and butter.

Yield: 4 to 6 servings

Spring Garden Peas

1 quart fresh peas, shelled	1 tablespoon butter
½ cup water	1 teaspoon fresh mint, chopped (optional)

Bring water to boil in saucepan. Add peas, turn down heat to medium and cover. Steam for 15 minutes or until tender and bright green in appearance. Do not overcook. Drain and toss with butter, and mint if desired. Serve immediately.

Yield: 4 to 6 servings

Brandied Carrots

2 bunches carrots, scraped and sliced thinly	¾ teaspoon sugar
½ cup melted butter	½ teaspoon salt
	¼ cup brandy

Parboil carrots for 10 minutes or until slightly tender. Place carrots in large casserole in a thin layer. Combine melted butter, sugar, salt and brandy. Pour over carrots. Cover casserole and bake 30 minutes in 325° oven.

Yield: 8 servings

Spring Garden Salad

1 large head of lettuce   6 small spring onions
1 cucumber   8 or more radishes

Tear lettuce in bite-sized pieces. Slice onions, cucumber and radishes in thin slices. Be sure all vegetables are very crisp. Just before serving, toss with the following dressing:

Dressing:

1 teaspoon sugar   ½ cup vinegar
1 tablespoon flour   1 tablespoon butter
2 eggs   1 cup cold water
1 teaspoon mustard   ½ cup sweet cream
Pinch of salt and pepper

Mix sugar and flour; add beaten eggs, mustard, water, salt, pepper and vinegar and boil until thick. Add the butter while boiling. When this is cold, add the cream. Loose leaf lettuce, home grown, is much better to use than head lettuce.

Yield: 6 to 8 servings

Dandelion Greens

2 pounds large dandelion greens   ½ cup mushrooms, diced
2½ cups boiling water   2 strips bacon
½ cup celery, chopped   2 teaspoons sugar (optional)
½ cup onions, diced   ½ teaspoon pepper

Cut the roots and seeding flowers off the plants. Wash the greens and flowers several times, as left-over dirt may make the greens gritty to taste.

In a deep pot, add all of the ingredients to the boiling water except for the greens and pepper. Cover tightly and simmer until the celery is tender. Add the pepper and the dandelion greens. Simmer over low heat until the flowers are tender.

Yield: 4 to 6 servings

Greenfields Cabbage 'n' Potatoes

4 slices bacon
2 quarts boiling water
8 medium potatoes, quartered
1 medium or large cabbage,
    coarsely shredded

1 tablespoon parsley flakes
Dash of oregano flakes
Salt and pepper to taste

Boil the bacon for 15 minutes; remove from the water and discard. Add the remaining ingredients. Cover tightly and allow the vegetables to simmer over medium-low heat until the potatoes are tender.

Yield: 8 servings

 ## Cole Slaw

FROM THE ORDINARY

¼ cup vinegar
¼ cup sugar
⅓ cup mayonnaise

1 small firm cabbage, shredded
1 medium carrot, grated

In a small dish, combine the vinegar, sugar and mayonnaise; stir until the sugar is dissolved. Mix the cabbage and carrots in a large bowl. Pour the dressing over the vegetables. Mix and serve.

Yield: 6 to 8 servings

 *Potato Salad*

6 large potatoes

1 tablespoon celery seed or
   ½ stalk celery, finely minced

¼ cup sugar

1 cup mayonnaise

1 teaspoon salt

1 small onion, diced

1 whole sweet pimento, diced

1 teaspoon pepper

⅓ cup prepared mustard

1 cup sweet relish or
   1 sweet pickle, diced

Dice the potatoes and cook until tender. Drain, rinse with cold water and drain again. Add celery. Let cool for one hour. Mix together the remaining ingredients; stir gently into the diced potatoes.

Yield: 6 to 8 servings

Yuletide Corn Pudding

2 15-ounce cans corn, drained

2 8-ounce cans creamed corn

2 tablespoons flour

½ cup milk

1 teaspoon vanilla

3 tablespoons sugar

1 egg

½ teaspoon cinnamon

¼ teaspoon nutmeg

Drain corn and mix with creamed corn in dish. Sprinkle with 2 tablespoons flour and mix. In small bowl blend milk, vanilla, sugar, egg and spices to make custard. Ladle custard over corn and stir gently. Bake uncovered at 350° for about 50 minutes.

Yield: 8 servings

Cornmeal-Fried Okra

1 pound small okra

1 large egg

⅓ cup yellow cornmeal

2 tablespoons flour

½ teaspoon salt

pinch of ground red pepper

3 cups vegetable shortening
  for frying

Rinse okra and drain well. Trim off stems and slice into ½-inch pieces. In medium-sized bowl, beat egg lightly. In plastic food-storage bag, combine cornmeal, flour, ¼ teaspoon of salt and the red pepper. In heavy skillet or saucepan, heat shortening to 375° on deep-fat thermometer. Add okra to egg and toss to coat completely. Drop okra, a few at a time, into the cornmeal mixture and shake to coat. Place okra, a handful at a time, into hot shortening and fry 2–3 minutes until crisp and brown. With slotted spoon, remove and place on paper towels. Keep warm until all okra has been fried. Sprinkle with remaining salt and serve.

Yield: 4 to 6 servings

Pickled Okra

6 garlic cloves

6 hot red peppers

40 to 50 small okra

6 teaspoons dill seed

1 quart vinegar

1 cup water

½ cup non-iodized salt

Sterilize 6 pint jars. It is important to use only regular canning jars. Use whole spices, not ground. Place 1 garlic clove and 1 red pepper in each jar. Pack firmly with okra. Add 1 teaspoon dill seed to each jar. Boil vinegar, water and salt. Simmer for 5 minutes and pour immediately over okra. Seal. Store in a dark, cool place and allow pickles to "set" several weeks before serving.

Never use copper, brass or zinc utensils in canning.

Yield: 6 pints

Seafood

Oyster Pie with Chicken

5½ to 6 pound chicken, cut up

2 medium onions, quartered

2 teaspoons allspice

6 stalks celery with tops, diced

1 bay leaf

2 tablespoons parsley flakes

Salt and pepper to taste

20 small white onions

5 carrots, thinly sliced

1 pound green peas

3 medium potatoes, diced

1 pint oysters, drained

½ cup butter or margarine

1 egg, well-beaten

3 tablespoons milk

½ cup all-purpose flour

½ cup cream

Piecrust, see recipe on page 124

In a large pot, cover the chicken with 6 cups water. Add the quartered onions, allspice, ⅓ of the diced celery, bay leaf and parsley. Salt and pepper to taste. Cover and simmer for 90 minutes or until the meat is tender. Remove the meat from the broth; discard the skin and bone. Strain the broth, discarding the vegetables and saving the liquid. Return the broth to the pot. Add the onions, carrots, peas, potatoes and remaining celery. Boil for 30 minutes or until tender. Gradually add ½ cup of flour and stir constantly to avoid getting lumps. Add cream and stir until broth thickens. Dice the chicken as desired; mix with the oysters, cooked vegetables and broth. Pour into a casserole dish and cover with piecrust. Cut small slits in the crust to allow steam to escape. Mix the egg with the milk; brush the mix over the crust. Bake at 350° for 55 minutes or until the crust is golden brown.

Yield: 8 to 10 servings

Louisiana Seafood Gumbo

1½ pounds shrimp
½ cup celery tops
¼ cup butter
1 medium onion, diced
2 stalks celery, thinly sliced
1 small green pepper, diced
2¼ cups canned tomatoes
4 to 6 ounces tomato puree
3 tablespoons flour
½ cup okra

1 cup scallops
½ teaspoon garlic powder
1 bay leaf
1 teaspoon salt
1 teaspoon pepper
¾ teaspoon Worcestershire sauce
1 teaspoon thyme
1 teaspoon sassafras
½ cup crabmeat
¾ cup oysters

Clean the shrimp and set aside, reserving the shells. Mix the celery tops with the shells and 2 quarts water in a large kettle, bringing the liquid to a boil. Cook over medium-high heat for 40 minutes. Strain, saving the broth. Using 2 tablespoons butter, sauté the onions, celery and green peppers until the vegetables are tender. Add the tomatoes, tomato puree and half of the broth. Simmer for 30 minutes. Mix the flour with the remaining butter and add to the vegetable mixture until well-blended. Simmer over low heat for 12 minutes. Add the okra, shrimp, scallops, garlic powder, bay leaf, salt, pepper and Worcestershire sauce. Cover and cook for 30 minutes. Add the thyme and sassafras; stir continuously for 10 minutes, being careful not to boil the mixture. Add the crabmeat and oysters. Cover and simmer over low heat another 7 minutes. Serve over rice.

Yield: 6 to 8 servings

Seafood Gumbo

1 pound shrimp

1 cup boiling water, lightly salted

¼ cup vegetable oil

¼ cup flour

1 cup chopped celery

1 cup chopped onion

1 cup shallots

1 cup chopped green pepper

3 to 4 tomatoes, peeled and chopped up with all juice

1 pint oysters with liquid

1 pound crabmeat

1 cup fresh chopped parsley

2 cups sliced fresh okra

Dash hot sauce

Drop shrimp into boiling water and boil 1 to 2 minutes until shrimp turns pink. Do not over cook. Save liquid for gumbo. Peel shrimp and set aside. Combine oil and flour in stock pot. Cook over medium heat to make roux, stirring until thickened. Add celery, onion, shallots, bell pepper, tomatoes and juice, and shrimp broth. Cover and simmer until vegetables are tender. Stir in oysters with liquid, crabmeat, shrimp, parsley, okra, and hot sauce. Cook 5 to 6 minutes or until okra is tender. Serve as gumbo or over cooked rice.

Yield: 6 to 8 servings

New England Clam Chowder

½ cup bacon, chopped

½ cup onion, chopped

15 ounces minced clams

1¾ cups potatoes, diced

¾ teaspoon salt

4½ cups milk

2 sprigs parsley, finely chopped

Lightly fry the bacon and onions until the onions are tender. Drain the liquid from the clams; add the liquid to a pot with the potatoes and salt. Cover and cook over medium heat for 20 minutes or until the potatoes are tender. Add the clams and milk; allow to simmer for 5 minutes. Drain the bacon and onions; add to the soup and simmer for another 5 minutes. Sprinkle with parsley, and pour into bowls.

Yield: 10 servings

Granny's Middlebrook Stew

3 pounds fresh fish fillet

¼ cup olive oil

1 cup mushrooms, chopped

3 medium onions, finely chopped

6 lemons

8 egg yolks

6 tablespoons flour, sifted

1 tablespoon parsley flakes

1 teaspoon celery seed

1 teaspoon ginger

Drop the fish into 4 cups boiling water and ¼ cup olive oil. In a saucepan stew together the mushrooms and onions in 2 cups water until tender. Add to the fish. Take the juice from 6 lemons; strain and blend with the egg yolks at high speed for 2 minutes. Blend in the flour at medium speed for 2 minutes. When the fish is almost done, break the fish apart with a fork and then add the spices and the lemon-egg mixture. Allow to simmer, uncovered, until the fish is tender. Serve with additional lemon slices if desired.

Yield: 6 to 8 servings

Stewed Oysters

4 cups oysters

1 pint cream

1 pint whole milk

1 teaspoon pepper

¼ teaspoon celery seed

¼ teaspoon celery salt

¾ teaspoon salt

¼ cup butter

2 egg yolks, well-beaten

1 tablespoon parsley flakes

Drain the oysters; reserve the liquid. Combine the liquid with the cream and milk in a large pot. Simmer over low heat for 10 minutes. Do not allow the sauce to boil. Reduce the heat. Add the oysters and all spices excluding the parsley flakes. Simmer over low heat for 7 minutes, stirring constantly to prevent scorching. Add the butter, egg yolks and parsley flakes. Simmer for another 7 minutes. Serve.

Yield: 4 to 6 servings

Scalloped Oysters

4 cups coarse toast crumbs

½ cup melted butter

4 dozen raw oysters

½ cup oyster liquid

½ teaspoon salt

4 tablespoons cream

¼ teaspoon pepper

2 teaspoons Worcestershire sauce

Dash of cayenne pepper

4 tablespoons cream

4 tablespoons sherry or

    4 more tablespoons cream

Heat oven to 425°. Combine crumbs and butter. Use one third of the mixture to cover bottom of greased baking dish. Arrange half of oysters in crumbs. Combine oyster liquid, salt, cream, pepper and remaining ingredients. Spoon half over oysters. Sprinkle one third of crumbs on top with rest of oysters, then rest of sauce; then crumbs. Bake uncovered 30 to 40 minutes.

Yield: 8 servings

Baked Fish Cakes

2½ pounds perch or any firm,
    white fish

1 tablespoon oil

1 medium onion, diced

2 medium potatoes, shredded

½ cup red bell peppers, diced

¾ teaspoon salt

1 tablespoon Old Bay
    Seasoning*

¾ teaspoon paprika

2 eggs, beaten

2 cups bread crumbs

Bake fish on sheet pan at 350° for 20 minutes or until fish flakes with a fork. Let cool and then flake fish in a large bowl. Heat oil in saucepan. Cook onions until translucent. Add to fish in bowl along with vegetables, seasonings, eggs, and bread crumbs. Mix well to bind. Form mixture into 12 cakes and place on nonstick sheet pan. Bake at 350° for 15 to 20 minutes or until lightly browned.

Yield: 12 cakes

*This modern-day ingredient adds extra flavor to this older-day recipe.

Fried Soft Shell Crabs

8 medium soft shell crabs   1 cup flour

Salt and pepper to taste   Fat for frying

Soak crabs in cold, salt water for 30 minutes. Drain. Season with salt
and pepper. Dip crabs lightly in flour and pan fry in shallow, hot fat.
A combination of bacon drippings and oil adds to the taste of the crabs.
Cook 4 to 5 minutes on each side, depending on the size. Drain well.
Garnish with fresh parsley and lemon wedges.

Note: For easy cleaning of soft-shell crabs, lift up the pointed ends and
remove the spongy fingers, remove the face apron and all spongy material
underneath. Soak in water and thoroughly dry before cooking.

Yield: 8 servings

Steamed Mussels Tarragon

4 pounds mussels, scrubbed   1 tablespoon shallots, minced
   and debearded   ¼ cup fresh tarragon, chopped
8 ounces clam juice   1 teaspoon butter
½ cup white wine   ½ cup heavy cream
2–3 cloves garlic, minced

Combine wine, clam juice, garlic, shallots and mussels in a heavy saucepan
over medium heat. Cover and steam until mussels open. This should take
only 5–10 minutes. Check frequently or remove lid after a few minutes of
steaming. Use slotted spoon to place mussels in a serving bowl. Add butter
and cream to pan juices. Stir quickly to mix and pour over mussels Sprinkle
with tarragon and serve.

Yield: 4 servings

Grilled Salmon with Orange Marmalade

½ cup orange marmalade

2 teaspoons toasted sesame oil

2 teaspoons soy sauce

½ teaspoon fresh ginger, grated

1 garlic clove, minced

3 tablespoons rice vinegar

1 pound salmon fillet, cut in fourths

Combine marmalade, sesame oil, soy sauce, ginger and garlic and vinegar.
Heat grill. Brush orange glaze on each side of salmon and grill about
5 minutes on each side or until salmon flakes with a fork.

Yield: 4 servings

Baked Red Snapper with Crabmeat

½ cup lump crabmeat, cartilage removed

1 ripe plum tomato, seeded and diced

1 tablespoon fresh cilantro, chopped

½ teaspoon lime zest

freshly ground pepper to taste

1 tablespoon heavy cream

1 whole red snapper, 1½ to
   2 pounds, bone removed

2 thin lime wedges

vegetable oil for baking dish

In a bowl, combine crabmeat, tomatoes, cilantro, lime zest, and pepper.
Gently stir in cream to combine and bind mixture. Open snapper and
spread stuffing evenly along bottom layer. Close fish and secure with
toothpicks. Make 2 deep slits in fish, top to bottom and insert lime wedges.
Place fish in lightly oiled baking dish. Set in center of preheated oven and
bake at 350° for 25 to 30 minutes. Or until fish flakes with a fork. Remove
to a serving dish and garnish with more cilantro and limes.

Yield: 4 servings

Pan-fried Trout

½ cup buttermilk

1 egg

½ cup cornmeal

¼ cup flour

salt, pepper to taste

2 whole trout, ½ pound each, cleaned

2 tablespoons vegetable oil

1 tablespoon clarified butter

1 lemon, cut in half

Mix buttermilk and egg in bowl. Mix cornmeal, flour, salt and pepper in a shallow bowl or on a plate. Dip trout first in buttermilk mixture and then coat in cornmeal mixture, shaking off excess. Heat oil and clarified butter in a large nonstick skillet over medium-high heat. Add trout and reduce heat very slightly. Cook for about 4 to 5 minutes per side until golden brown and crisp. Serve immediately with lemon halves.

Yield: 2 servings

Note: To clarify butter, melt over low heat in a heavy saucepan. Remove from heat and let rest for 5 minutes. With a spoon, carefully remove the foamy white butterfat that has risen to the top. Discard fat. Slowly pour off the clear liquid and refrigerate. Discard the milky solids that remain on the bottom of the saucepan. Clarified butter will keep fro several weeks in the refrigerator. Because the water and milk solids are removed, it can be heated to higher temperatures without burning.

Poultry

# *Colonial Fried Chicken*

FROM THE ORDINARY

1 cup all-purpose flour	1 teaspoon pepper
1 teaspoon oregano	2- to 3-pound fryer, cut up
1 teaspoon garlic salt	3 cups shortening
1 teaspoon seasoning salt	

Combine flour and seasonings; roll the cut up chicken in the flour mixture. Using a Dutch oven or other heavy deep pan, fry in shortening at 350° for 12 to 15 minutes on each side, or until tender.

Yield: 6 servings

Virginia Captain

2 cups all-purpose flour	1 small green pepper, chopped
1 teaspoon salt	1 teaspoon minced garlic
1 teaspoon pepper	¼ teaspoon thyme
1 tablespoon parsley flakes	2 teaspoons curry powder
3½ pounds chicken, cut up	14 to 16 ounces stewed tomatoes
6 tablespoons butter or margarine	2½ tablespoons currant jelly
2 small onions, chopped	

Mix together the flour, salt, pepper and parsley flakes. Roll the chicken in the flour mix. Melt the butter in a large skillet; brown the chicken evenly on both sides; remove the chicken. Over low heat, sauté the onions, peppers, garlic, thyme and curry powder in the remaining butter; stir constantly to avoid scorching. Stir in the stewed tomatoes. Add the chicken, skin-side up. Cover and simmer for 30 minutes. Stir in the jelly, blending thoroughly with the sauce. Put all into a greased casserole dish. Cover and bake at 450° for 25 minutes or until the chicken is tender.

Yield: 4 to 6 servings

Chicken Pudding

Chicken giblets

2 small onions, peeled

4 celery tops

½ teaspoon thyme

3 sprigs parsley

2 cloves

2 teaspoons pepper

2 teaspoons garlic salt

1½ cups all-purpose flour

½ stick butter

4- to 6-pound chicken, cut up

3 eggs

1 cup whole milk

½ teaspoon salt

Paprika

In a saucepan, cover the giblets with water. Add the onion, celery, thyme, parsley, cloves and 1 teaspoon each of pepper and garlic salt. Cover and cook over low heat for 1 hour and 15 minutes; strain, saving the broth and giblets.

Mix 1 teaspoon pepper and 1 teaspoon garlic salt with the flour. In a skillet, heat 2 tablespoons butter. Roll the chicken in the flour and brown in the butter. Mix the chicken with the broth in a large pot. Cook over medium low heat until the meat is tender, adding water as necessary. Remove the chicken from the broth and place in a large casserole dish.

In a mixing bowl, blend the eggs, milk and 1 cup flour with the salt and remaining 2 tablespoons of butter; beat until creamy. Pour the batter over the meat in the casserole dish. Garnish as desired with paprika. Bake at 375° for 30 minutes or until the batter turns golden brown.

Yield: 4 to 6 servings

Chicken and Biscuits

1 4- to 5-pound stewing chicken,
  cut up
2 ribs celery, chopped
1 small onion, chopped
1 teaspoon salt

¼ teaspoon white pepper
4½ tablespoons flour
uncooked biscuits, see page 10
  for recipe

Simmer chicken, celery and onions in 3 to 4 cups of water until chicken is tender and pulls away from bone. Discard skin and bones and cut chicken into medium-sized pieces. Reduce stock to 2½ cups and remove excess fat. Thicken stock with flour which has been mixed with 6 tablespoons of water. Salt and pepper to taste. Place chicken pieces in bottom of 12 x 8 x 2½-inch baking dish or 2 quart dish. Pour gravy over chicken and let cool. Place uncooked biscuits on topped of cooked chicken and bake at 350° for 25 to 30 minutes until biscuits are done.

Yield: 6 to 8

Chicken Breasts Florentine

4 boneless chicken breasts with skin	Parmesan cheese
salt, pepper to taste	2 cups mushrooms, thinly sliced
1 pound spinach leaves	3 tablespoons shallots, finely chopped
4 tablespoons butter	⅛ teaspoon nutmeg
	4 tablespoons freshly grated

Sprinkle chicken with salt and pepper and set aside. Pick over spinach leaves to remove tough stems and blemished leaves. Rinse in cold water and drain well. Heat 2 tablespoons of butter in heavy skillet and add the chicken breasts skin side down. Cook until nicely browned, about two minutes on each side. Remove chicken and set aside. Keep warm. Add the remaining butter to the skillet with the mushrooms, shallots, and salt and pepper to taste. Cook, stirring often, until mushrooms give up their liquid and liquid is almost evaporated. Add the spinach and cook until wilted. Stir in nutmeg.

Cut four squares of heavy duty aluminum foil, large enough to hold a piece of chicken and spinach mixture securely. Spoon equal portions of the spinach mixture onto the center of each square. Sprinkle each portion with one tablespoon of cheese. Top with one piece of chicken, skin side up. Close foil packet tightly. Place packets in baking dish and bake at 425° for 25 minutes.

Sauce:

2 tablespoons butter	½ cup heavy cream
2 tablespoons flour	juice of half a lemon
1¼ cups rich chicken broth	salt, pepper to taste

Melt the butter in a saucepan. Add the flour and stir with a wire whisk. Add the broth and stir until mixture is thickened. Set aside to cool about five minutes. Add the cream, lemon juice, salt and pepper. The sauce is ready to be served. You may want to keep warm or reheat in the saucepan before serving.

When chicken is done, open packages and spoon spinach then chicken onto plates. Spoon sauce over chicken. Extra sauce may be served separately.

Yield: 4 servings

Chestnut Filling for Turkey

1 quart large chestnuts	2 cups soft bread crumbs
¼ melted butter	2 tablespoons chopped celery
1 tablespoon finely chopped parsley	1 teaspoon salt
½ teaspoon pepper	2 eggs, beaten

Shell chestnuts then boil in two quarts of salted water. Boil until tender (time depends on age of chestnuts). Drain and mash through a coarse strainer. Sauté bread crumbs and celery in butter. Add parsley, salt and pepper to taste, and well-beaten eggs. Add to chestnut mixture. Mix well and stuff into turkey. Be sure to close the cavity. Cook according to directions for stuffed turkey.

Roast Turkey with Mushroom Stuffing

½ cup butter

1 can pitted black olives, drained and halved

3 medium onions, chopped

2 cups mushrooms, sliced

3 large stalks celery, chopped

3 loaves stuffing bread, cut into crouton-size cubes

1¼ cups seasoned bread crumbs

1 teaspoon parsley flakes

1 teaspoon oregano flakes

1 teaspoon salt

1 teaspoon pepper

1 teaspoon garlic salt

1½ cups cooking wine

20- to 22-pound turkey

In a frying pan, melt the butter and sauté the olives, onions, mushrooms and celery. In a large, shallow roasting pan (about 4 to 5 inches deep) mix the bread cubes, crumbs and spices. Add the ingredients from the frying pan; add the wine and mix well. Stuff the turkey, closing the cavity by placing skewers across it and lacing with a cord. Tie the drumsticks to the tail. Place the turkey, breast-side up, in the roasting pan. Grease the bird thoroughly and cover with aluminum foil. Bake at 325°. After baking for 6½ hours, cut the cord tying the drumsticks to the tail. Bake an additional hour (total 7½ hours) and uncover the turkey. Bake for one more hour. The turkey will be done when the drumsticks can be easily moved and twisted out of joint. If using a meat thermometer, insert the prong into the center of the inside of the thigh, close to the cavity. The thermometer should read 190 to 195° when the turkey is done.

Yield: 24 servings

Roast Turkey with Oyster Stuffing

3 medium onions

1 carrot, sliced thin

1 tablespoon parsley flakes

¼ teaspoon celery seed

1¼ teaspoons salt

1 teaspoon allspice

1 bay leaf

4 stalks celery

10 to 12 pounds turkey with giblets

2 pounds white bread, cubed

¼ to ½ cup chopped parsley

Dash thyme

Dash sage

1 teaspoon pepper

½ cup mushrooms, sliced
 (optional)

1½ cups butter

1 pint oysters

1 egg, well-beaten

2 teaspoons lemon juice

Quarter 1 onion and add to 3 to 4 cups water; add the carrot, parsley flakes, celery seed, salt, allspice, bay leaf, 1 stalk of celery and the giblets. Cover and cook over medium heat for 10 minutes. Reduce to low heat; cover and simmer for 2 hours. Strain, saving only the broth and giblets. Chop up the giblets.

Preheat the oven to 325°. In a large, shallow roasting pan, mix the bread with the chopped parsley, spices and giblets. Dice the remaining onions and celery. Sauté the onions, celery and mushrooms in 1 cup of butter until the onions are transparent. Add the oysters, egg, lemon juice and sautéed mixture to the bread; mix thoroughly. Lightly salt the inside of the turkey; stuff and sew up. Place the turkey in the shallow roasting pan, breast-side up. Grease the bird with ¼ cup butter. Salt the skin as desired and garnish with paprika. Bake for approximately 5½ hours or until the drumsticks can be easily twisted out of joint. The bird should remain covered with aluminum foil for the first 4½ hours. When the turkey is done, place the bird on a platter and return to the oven to keep warm.

For the gravy, skim off most of the grease from the drippings. Combine the reserved broth and drippings; boil, stirring constantly. Cream together the remaining ¼ cup butter with 6 tablespoons flour. Add the creamed mixture to the broth and continue to stir until well-blended. Simmer over low heat for 5 to 10 minutes. Season the gravy as desired.

Yield: 12 to 14 servings

Giblet Gravy

2 tablespoons vegetable oil
  or unsalted butter
Turkey giblets
2 stalks celery, chopped
1 large onion, chopped

3 quarts turkey or chicken stock
2 teaspoons cornstarch
½ cup water
Salt and pepper, to taste

Heat oil or butter in a baking pan. Add giblets, celery, and onion, and roast in oven beside turkey for 30 minutes. Bring turkey stock to boil in saucepan; add browned giblets and vegetables with the pan juices and simmer 45 minutes, until liquid is reduced by one-third. Strain stock, return to saucepan and keep warm over low heat.

Blend cornstarch with cold water. Add to stock and heat, stirring constantly, until thickened. Season with salt and pepper.

Yield: 8 cups

Cornbread Dressing

¾ cup flour	1¼ cups corn meal
2½ teaspoons baking powder	1 egg
1 tablespoon sugar	3 tablespoons melted butter
½ teaspoon salt	1 cup milk

Sift together flour, baking powder, sugar and salt. Add cornmeal. Beat egg in separate bowl with butter and milk. Combine all ingredients with a few quick strokes. Pour batter into greased pan and bake at 425° for 15 minutes or until cornbread is done in middle. Cool cornbread and crumble into large bowl.

1 cup chopped celery	2 eggs, beaten
¼ cup chopped onion	1 teaspoon pepper
¼ cup melted butter, divided	2½ cups turkey or chicken broth

Sauté celery and onions in 2 tablespoons of butter until soft. Add to crumbled cornbread. Add other ingredients and mix to soft consistency. Pour into greased 9" x 9" baking pan and bake at 400° until brown, about one hour.

Yield: 9 servings

Roast Burgundy Goose

12-pound goose
salt, pepper to taste
2 cloves garlic, minced

2 oranges, quartered
6 thin strips salt pork

Wash and dry goose thoroughly, inside and out. Pat to dry. Using a two-tined fork, prick skin all over bird. Sprinkle breast with salt, pepper, and garlic and bring to room temperature. In cavity, place orange quarters, squeezing them slightly. Place strips of salt pork on breast of goose and put bird on rack in open roasting pan. Bake at 325° for one hour. Drain off excess fat. Increase heat to 350° and continue roasting for three hours. During this cooking period, you will have to pour off excess fat at least two times. You may even want to change roasting pans. During the last hour of cooking, you will find that most of the fat has left the bird. Now is the time to baste with Burgundy wine. This will give a fine aroma, so baste often, adding more wine if needed.

Yield: 10 to 12 servings

Stewed Pheasant

3 3-pound pheasants
4 stalks celery, diced
8 medium onions, quartered
1 bouillon cube, chicken flavor
Salt and pepper to taste
8 potatoes, quartered
½ cup barley
1 cup rice

2 cups stewed tomatoes
3 medium (6 to 8 inches long)
  summer squash, thinly sliced
4 cups corn
1 teaspoon celery salt
1 tablespoon Worcestershire sauce
3 sprigs parsley, lightly chopped

Wash the pheasants thoroughly; combine with the celery, onions, bouillon, salt and pepper in 2 quarts boiling water. Boil for 15 minutes. Reduce to low heat. Cover and simmer for 1½ hours or until the pheasant is tender. Remove the birds. Add the potatoes, barley and rice; cover and simmer until the rice and potatoes are tender.

Bone the pheasant, discarding the skin. Dice the meat as desired and return to the broth. Add the tomatoes, squash, corn, celery salt and Worcestershire sauce. Simmer for an additional 15 minutes. Garnish with the freshly chopped parsley and serve.

Yield: 8 to 10 servings

Smothered Quail

12 quail
½ cup butter
¼ cup plus 1 tablespoon
  all-purpose flour

2 cups chicken broth
½ cup sherry
Salt and black pepper

Saute quail in butter in heavy skillet, turning to brown on all sides. Place in baking dish. Blend flour with butter in skillet. Gradually add broth, sherry, salt and black pepper. Mix well. Pour over quail. Bake, covered, at 350° for 1 hour. Serve with wild rice.

Yield: 6 servings

Roast Duck

6-pound duckling	Paprika
½ loaf stuffing bread, cubed	Salt and pepper to taste
¼ teaspoon cinnamon	2 oranges
¼ teaspoon nutmeg	¼ cup seedless raisins, chopped
¼ teaspoon allspice	3 tablespoons pineapple juice
½ teaspoon sugar	¼ cup butter, melted

Wash the duck thoroughly; dab dry with a paper towel inside and out.
Mix together the bread and seasonings in a shallow roasting pan. Peel one
orange; cut up into small pieces and add to the dry ingredients. Mix in the
chopped raisins, pineapple juice and butter. Lightly salt the cavity of the
bird, then stuff. Place the duck, breast-side up, on a rack in the pan. Pour
2½ cups water over the bird. Slice the other orange; stick the slices into
place on the sides and top of the bird with tooth picks. Garnish to taste
with paprika, salt and pepper. Cover lightly with aluminum foil. Roast the
bird at 350° for 1½ hours. Remove the foil and roast another 20 minutes.

Yield: 4 to 6 servings

Broiled Duck Breasts with Red Currant Sauce

½ cup dry red wine or sherry	½ teaspoon crushed thyme
¼ cup soy sauce	¼ teaspoon freshly ground pepper
¼ cup vegetable oil	4 duck breasts, skinned and boned

Combine wine, soy sauce, oil, pepper and thyme in small bowl, stirring well.
Place duck breasts in a shallow bowl or dish; pour marinade over meat.
Cover tightly and refrigerate 2 to 3 hours, turning duck occasionally.

Remove duck breasts from marinade and place on broiler rack. Broil
5 inches from heat 15 to 20 minutes, turning once. Thinly slice and serve
with sauce. See recipe on page 112.

Yield: 4 servings

Meats

Roast Venison or Deer

Venison is the meat of a deer. It should be hung up to ripen for several days before using. The saddle or loin is the choicest cut for roasting; plenty of fat is an indication of the excellence of the meat. The haunch is also roasted. It should always be cooked rare. Wipe the meat with a cloth that has been wrung out of weak vinegar. The meat is improved by larding but instead it may be spread with melted butter. Sprinkle with salt and cook in a hot oven 450° for ½ hour. Reduce the temperature to moderate 350° and allow 15 minutes to the pound for a saddle, and 20 minutes for a haunch. Turn the meat over when half done and dredge lightly with flour and salt. When flour begins to brown spread the meat with currant jelly and add a little water to the pan. Baste often. Serve hot with currant jelly. A roast of venison may be sprinkled with minced onion and lemon juice before being put in the oven.

Venison Roast

¼ pound salt pork	1 cup crushed seasoned croutons
5 to 6 pounds venison roast	½ teaspoon parsley flakes
10 strips bacon	1 lemon, quartered (optional)
1 large onion chopped	2 tablespoons Worcestershire sauce
3 stalks celery, thinly sliced	Salt and pepper to taste
2 cups mushrooms, sliced	

Boil the salt pork in 2½ cups water for 20 minutes. Discard the pork and save the broth. Remove all excess fat from the roast. Lay 7 strips bacon on the bottom of a roasting pan. Place the meat over the bacon. Garnish the top of the roast with the remaining strips. Pour the boiled water over the meat. Add the onions, celery and mushrooms. Sprinkle the crushed croutons and parsley flakes over all. Squeeze the lemon pieces, allowing the juice to run over the meat. Add the lemon rinds to the pan. Pour the Worcestershire sauce over the roast. Salt and pepper as desired. Cover and bake at 325° for 2½ hours or until done. Baste and add water as necessary.

Yield: 10 servings

Back Country Roast Leg of Lamb

6 pound leg of lamb	1 teaspoon lemon pepper
8 medium potatoes	½ cup all-purpose flour*
6 medium onions	½ teaspoon celery salt
2 small yellow turnips (optional)	½ teaspoon parsley flakes
12 medium carrots	3 springs fresh parsley,
Salt and pepper to taste	lightly chopped

Trim the excess fat from the roast, setting off to one side. (See note at bottom of recipe.) Peel and quarter the potatoes, onions and turnips. Peel the carrots and cut into 2 inch lengths. Place the leg of lamb into a roasting pan with the vegetables on all sides and on top. Pour 6 to 8 cups water over the roast. Sprinkle with salt, pepper and lemon pepper as desired. Cover the pan tightly with aluminum foil. Bake the lamb at 325° for 2 hours or 20 to 25 minutes per pound.

Remove the roast from the pan, centering the meat on a large platter. Save drippings from pan. Assemble the vegetables around the meat; cover with the foil and return to the oven to keep warm.

Blend the flour into 1 cup water until smooth. Add the flour mixture, celery salt and parsley flakes to the drippings, stirring frequently over low heat for 20 minutes. When the gravy is done, remove the roast from the oven and garnish with the chopped parsley. Serve.

Yield: 8 servings

* You may need to adjust amount of flour depending on the amount of drippings in the pan. If the gravy is thin, add more flour until you get the desired consistency.

Note: Uncooked lamb fat makes an excellent water repellent for leather work boots; just rub the fat into the leather. Freeze the remaining fat for later use.

Irish Stew

2 pounds mutton
6 onions
1 carrot, sliced

8 medium potatoes, cut thick
Salt and pepper to taste

Cut up mutton. Remove some fat and place the meat in a saucepan with 1½ pints hot water. Add 6 onions and 1 carrot sliced. Cook very gently. Simmer for 1 hour and then add 8 medium sized potatoes cut in thick pieces. Season to taste with salt and pepper. Cook until potatoes are tender.

Yield: 8 servings

Lemon Veal

1½ pounds veal round steak,
  ¾-inch thick
2 tablespoons butter or margarine
½ cup chicken broth

3 tablespoons fresh lemon juice
Salt and pepper to taste
1 teaspoon fresh parsley, chopped

Melt butter in skillet. Add veal and brown on both sides. Add chicken broth, lemon juice, salt and pepper. Cover and bring to boil. Reduce heat and simmer for 30 minutes, turning veal steaks halfway through cooking. Remove cover, stir in parsley and serve with pan juices.

Yield: 4 servings

Highland Shepherd Pie

8 medium potatoes, peeled
   and quartered
½ cup milk
Leftovers: lamb, turkey, chicken
   or pot roast with the vegetables
   and gravy

1 cup corn
Butter
Paprika
Salt and pepper to taste

Cook the potatoes until tender; mash with the milk. Using half of the mashed potatoes, line a greased baking dish on the sides and bottom. Fill with the left-over vegetables, meat and gravy. Sprinkle the corn over the top. Smooth out and cover the ingredients with the remaining mashed potatoes. Place 8 pats butter, 2 inches apart, on the mashed potato top. Season with paprika, salt and pepper to taste. Bake at 325° for 45 minutes or until the potatoes form a light golden brown crust.

Yield: 6 to 8 servings

Hare-Ricing Stew (Rabbit)

3 medium onions, diced
2 medium peppers, diced
1 stalk celery, diced
1 teaspoon salt
1 teaspoon pepper
5 cups water
1 cup green olives

1 tablespoon sugar (optional)
1 tablespoon oregano flakes
12 ounces tomato sauce
12 ounces tomato paste
2 rabbits, dressed (approximately
   4 to 5 pounds)
1½ cups rice

Over medium heat, mix together the onions, peppers, celery, salt, pepper, water, olives, sugar and oregano. Simmer for ½ hour, stirring occasionally. Add the tomato sauce and paste; add the rabbit. Cook for 45 minutes, tightly covered. Add the rice and cook for another 45 minutes or until the meat is tender.

Yield: 6 servings

Mrs. Michie's Brunswick Stew

1 tablespoon oil

1 large onion, chopped

1 tablespoon garlic, diced

¾ cup flour

5 cups chicken broth

1 ham hock

1 teaspoon salt

¼ teaspoon pepper

1 tablespoon thyme

2 pounds chicken, cooked, diced

4 cups tomatoes, crushed

4 cups potatoes, cubed

1½ cups lima beans

1½ cups corn

½ cup peas

1 teaspoon sugar

Heat oil in a large soup pot. Cook onion and garlic until translucent. Stir in flour gradually and add chicken broth, ham hock, salt, pepper, and thyme. Stir well. Add rest of ingredients and simmer over low heat for 45 minutes. Stew tastes better the next day.

Yield: 8 to 10 servings

Old-Fashioned Meat Loaf

1 pound ground beef

½ pound ground veal, turkey or pork

¾ cup cracker or bread crumbs

½ cup diced celery

½ cup diced onion

¼ cup minced parsley

½ teaspoon salt

¼ teaspoon pepper

½ cup water

1 egg, slightly beaten

Combine meats; stir well. Add cracker crumbs and next seven ingredients; stir well. Press into a 9" x 6" loaf pan, and bake at 350° for 1 hour and 20 minutes. Holding meat loaf securely in place, tilt pan and drain any extra fat.

Yield: 8 servings

Chili Con Carne

2 cups celery, chopped

1 large onion, chopped

1 bell pepper, chopped

2 tablespoons vegetable oil

1 pound ground beef

1 28-ounce can of chopped tomatoes

6 ounces tomato paste

2 14-ounce cans red kidney beans

1 tablespoon chili powder

1 teaspoon cumin

Salt and pepper to taste

Brown celery, onions and bell peppers in oil until tender. Add ground beef and cook until well done. Drain fat. Add tomatoes, tomato paste, chili powder, cumin and pepper. Simmer for about 1 hour. Add beans and cook about 15 minutes longer. Serve with crackers or over rice.

Yield: 6 to 8 servings

Beef Stroganoff

1½ pounds fillet of beef

3 tablespoons butter

1 tablespoon grated onion

¾ pound sliced mushrooms

Salt to taste

Pepper to taste

Grated nutmeg to taste

½ teaspoon basil

¼ cup white wine

1 cup sweet or cultured sour cream

Cut fillet of beef into ½-inch slices. Pound them with a mallet until thin. Cut into strips about 1 inch wide. Melt 1 tablespoon butter in a pan. Sauté grated onion in the butter for about 2 minutes. Sauté the beef quickly in the butter for about 5 minutes. Turn so that it will be browned evenly. Remove beef and keep hot. Add 2 tablespoons butter to the pan. Stir in sliced mushrooms and sauté them in the butter. Add the beef. Season with salt and pepper, a grating of nutmeg, and the basil. Add and heat, but do not boil, ¼ cup white wine, 1 cup warm, sweet or cultured sour cream. Serve over noodles.

Yield: 6 servings

Homestyle Pot Roast

4-pound boneless chuck roast

1 large garlic clove, crushed

¼ cup flour

1 teaspoon pepper

2 tablespoons vegetable oil

¼ cup red wine

1 teaspoon coarsely-ground
pepper

1 10½-ounce can beef broth,
undiluted

1 bay leaf, crushed

1 teaspoon dried thyme

1 teaspoon dried oregano

2–3 large onions, quartered

12 baby carrots

12 small new potatoes, unpeeled

Rub roast with crushed garlic. Combine flour and pepper; dredge meat in flour mixture. Brown roast on all sides in hot oil in Dutch oven. Stir together wine and next five ingredients. Pour over roast. Cover and bake at 350° for 1 hour. Cooking times may vary depending on oven and quality of meat. Add vegetables, cover and bake for 1–2 hours until roast is tender.

Yield: 8 to 10 servings

Country Style Steak

2 tablespoons vegetable oil

4 cube steaks

1 cup flour, plus 2 tablespoons

salt, pepper to taste

½ cup water

Sprinkle salt and pepper on both sides of steaks. Dredge in 1 cup of flour. Heat oil in skillet. Brown on both sides. Remove steak from pan. Add enough flour to pan, about 2 tablespoons, to absorb pan liquids. Add ½ cup water and stir to make gravy. Add more water if necessary to reach desired consistency. Put steaks back in gravy, cover skillet and steam at medium heat until done. Turn steaks once during cooking.

Yield: 4 servings

Steak au Poivre

2 tablespoons peppercorns

4 steaks or filets

2 tablespoons peanut oil

3 tablespoons butter

2 tablespoon shallots, minced

½ cup wine

½ cup cream

Crush peppercorns. Press down on both sides of meat. Heat peanut oil in skillet. When hot, add steaks. Cook 3 minutes each side. Remove from pan and keep warm. Pour fat from skillet, but do not scrape pan. Add 2 tablespoons of butter and the shallots. Cook until shallots are wilted. Add wine, stir until reduced. Add cream and cook over high for one minute. Swirl in remaining butter. If steaks need cooking further, place in pan with sauce, cover, and steam until done. Spoon sauce over steaks.

Yield: 4 servings

Grilled Flank Steak

¼ cup soy sauce

2 teaspoons crushed thyme

2 tablespoons cream

2 tablespoons white wine mustard

½ teaspoon freshly ground
   black pepper

2 teaspoons fresh or dried ginger

1 2-pound flank steak

Combine all ingredients but the steak to make a marinade. Cover steak with marinade and cover for at least 2 to 3 hours. Reserve marinade. Heat grill. Cook steak on both sides for about 8 minutes each, while basting with marinade. Cooking times may vary according to thickness of steak. Slice diagonally against the grain.

Yield: 4 to 6 servings

Beef Tenderloin

1 5-pound beef tenderloin	¼ cup soy sauce
1 teaspoon garlic salt	½ cup butter
1 cup Burgundy wine	1 teaspoon lemon pepper

Place tenderloin on a lightly greased shallow roasting pan. Sprinkle with garlic salt. Bake at 425° for 10 minutes. Combine wine, soy sauce, butter and lemon pepper in a small saucepan. Cook until mixture is thoroughly heated. Pour over tenderloin. Bake an additional 30 to 40 minutes or until a thermometer registers 150 to 160°. Baste occasionally with pan drippings.

Yield: 10 servings

Red Flannel Hash

3 pounds corned beef, chopped (cooked)	½ cup heavy cream
6 potatoes, cooked and chopped	1 teaspoon salt
8 beets, cooked and chopped	1 teaspoon pepper
½ cup butter or margarine	1 teaspoon parsley flakes
2 medium or 1 large onion, diced	4 eggs, poached (optional)

In a large bowl, mix the corned beef, potatoes and beets. Melt half of the butter in the skillet and sauté the onions until tender. Add the onions, with the cream and seasonings, to the bowl; mix together well. In the same skillet, melt the remaining butter over low heat. Add the mixture and pat down flat with a spatula. Cover and cook for ½ hour or until the hash is well-browned. Slide the hash out of the skillet onto a platter. Fold over like an omelet. Garnish the top with the poached eggs.

Yield: 8 to 10 servings

Pork Chops and Apples

3 tablespoons butter

4 pork chops, 1 inch thick

2 apples

½ cup raisins, optional

½ teaspoon cinnamon

Quickly brown chops on both sides in 2 tablespoons butter. Remove chops from stove. Core unpeeled apples and slice into thin, circular pieces to cover bottom of baking dish twice. Add raisins, if desired. Sprinkle cinnamon over apples and dot with butter. Place pork chops on top. Cover and bake at 350° for 1½ hours.

Yield: 4 servings

Rosemary Pork Tenderloin

½ cup sherry

½ cup soy sauce

2 cloves garlic, crushed

1 tablespoon dry mustard

1 teaspoon fresh or dry ginger

1 tablespoon fresh rosemary, chopped

3 pork tenderloins

Combine all ingredients, except the pork tenderloins, and stir to mix. Place mixture in a closed dish with the tenderloins and allow to marinate at room temperature for 2 to 3 hours. Place tenderloins in a shallow baking dish. Pour a little of the marinade over top. Cook uncovered at 350° for 40 minutes or until temperature reaches 160 to 165°. Continue to baste with additional marinade and pan juices while cooking. Let sit for 15 minutes before slicing.

Yield: 8 servings

Baked Virginia Ham

4 cups apple cider

2 tablespoons brown sugar

2 medium onions, chopped

10 to 12 pound pre-cooked ham

2 dozen cloves

3 tablespoons all-purpose flour

¼ cup lemon juice

Combine 1 cup boiling water with the cider; add the brown sugar and the onions; boil for 8 minutes. Remove the rind from the ham. Score the meat and insert the cloves. Put the ham in a roasting pan. Strain the boiled mixture and pour over the ham. Bake at 325° for 1½ hours, basting every 20 minutes.

When the ham is done, pour the drippings into a frying pan. Brown the flour; stir in the lemon juice. Stir the sauce until thick and smooth.

Yield: 10 to 12 servings

 Virginia Country Ham

1 18- to 20-pound Virginia ham

3 cups brown sugar

2½ cups molasses

Prepare ham: scrub to remove the coating of seasonings, cover it with water, and soak for 24 hours. Place the ham, skin down, in a pan with enough fresh water to cover. Add brown sugar and molasses, bring to a boil, reduce heat and simmer, covered, for 5½ hours. Temperature should have reached 165°. If not, continue boiling until temperature is reached. When fully cooked, skin the ham and trim off excess fat.

Yield: 36 to 40 servings

Note: At Michie Tavern, we serve country ham at our Yuletide dinners with Murphy's Biscuits (page 10) and raisin sauce (page 111).

Sauces & More

Cheddar Cheese Sauce

2 tablespoons butter or margarine

1½ teaspoons onion,
   finely chopped (optional)

2 tablespoons flour

1¾ cups light cream

2 cups cheddar cheese, grated

¼ teaspoon paprika

¼ teaspoon salt

¼ teaspoon pepper

Melt the butter or margarine over low heat; add the onions and sauté. Stir in the flour; add the cream to make a sauce. Add the cheese and seasonings, stirring continuously over low heat until the cheese is melted. Serve hot over your favorite vegetables. Or, if allowed to cool, may be used as a cheese spread.

Yield: 2½ cups

Joshua's Bechamel Sauce

4 tablespoons butter or margarine

1 medium onion, grated

4 tablespoons flour

2 chicken bouillon cubes, crushed

2 cups hot milk

½ teaspoon parsley flakes

Salt and pepper to taste

In a saucepan, melt the butter or margarine; add the onion and heat, but do not brown. Blend in the flour. Remove from the heat. In ¼ cup boiling water, dissolve the crushed bouillon. Add the bouillon and the hot milk to the sauce; beat rapidly until the sauce is smooth. Return to medium heat. Stir continuously until the sauce boils; add the spices and simmer for 5 minutes. Strain (optional) and serve.

Yield: approximately. 2½ cups

French Cream Sauce

2 tablespoons butter

2 tablespoons shallots, chopped

¼ cup vinegar

2 tablespoons lemon juice

2 tablespoons white wine

1 cup heavy cream

Melt 1 tablespoon butter in saucepan. Add chopped shallots and cook slowly just until softened. Add vinegar, lemon juice and wine to saucepan. Cook down until you have about 2 tablespoons of liquid left. Add cream and stir constantly over low heat. When mixture begins to thicken, stir in remaining butter to melt.

Yield: 1 cup

Hollandaise Sauce

4 large egg yolks

1 cup butter

Juice of 1 large lemon

Beat egg yolks in top of double boiler over medium high heat. Do not let water boil or touch the bottom of the double boiler pan. Beat until thick and lemon-colored. Add about 3 tablespoons of butter at a time and beat thoroughly after each addition. When sauce has thickened, beat in lemon juice. Let cool to room temperature and beat before serving, or reheat in top of double boiler.

Herb Butter

1 teaspoon basil

1 teaspoon thyme

1 teaspoon tarragon

1 teaspoon chives

1 teaspoon rosemary

1 cup butter, softened

Use fresh or dried herbs. Chop or crumble and cream into butter. Serve on freshly baked bread.

Yield: 1 cup

Early Day Barbecue Sauce

¼ cup butter or margarine

3 tablespoons clove garlic, minced

¼ cup green peppers, minced

¾ cup onion, finely chopped

1¼ cups tomato sauce

¾ cup dry sherry

2 tablespoons light brown sugar

1 teaspoon dry mustard

3 teaspoons lemon juice

½ cup vinegar

2 teaspoons Worcestershire sauce

½ cup water

In a saucepan, melt the butter or margarine; sauté the garlic, peppers and onions. Add the remaining ingredients; mix and boil for 2 minutes, stirring continuously. Lower the heat and simmer for 45 minutes, stirring frequently to prevent scorching.

Yield: 3 to 4 cups

Carter Mountain Apple Butter Spread

7 quarts apple cider

12 pounds apples, peeled, pared and quartered

8 cups sugar

3 tablespoons cinnamon

2 tablespoons ground cloves

2 tablespoons allspice

Boil the cider for 30 minutes. Cook the apples in the boiling cider until tender. Remove the apples; mash in a large pot. Add the spices to the mashed apples. Stir over medium-low heat until the mixture becomes a soft paste. Remove from the heat. Seal in jars and store in a cool, dry place.

Yield: 20 8-ounce jars

Spiced Crab Apples

2 cups sugar

3 medium cinnamon sticks

4½ cups crab apples, peeled,
  pared and quartered

2 cups vinegar

9 whole cloves

Combine the sugar, cinnamon, vinegar and cloves in a large pot. Boil for 6 minutes, constantly stirring to blend well. Add the crab apples and boil again for 30 seconds. Simmer over low heat for 10 minutes or until the apples are tender. Let the ingredients cool. Cover the pot and store in a cold, dry place for 24 hours. Remove the crab apples. Boil the liquid until a thick syrup forms. Mix the apples with the syrup; store in jars well-sealed.

Yield: 6 8-ounce jars

Aunt Martha's Brandied Peaches

1 dozen peaches

8 dozen cloves

3 cups cold water

3 cups granulated sugar

2 small cinnamon sticks

¼ to ½ teaspoon mace

2½ cups brandy

10 8-ounce jars

In a pot of boiling water, cook the peaches for approximately 1 minute. Remove the peaches; peel and quarter. Stud each quarter with a couple of cloves. In a large saucepan, mix the peaches with the cold water, sugar and spices; bring to a boil, stirring frequently. Simmer over low heat for 22 minutes or until the peaches are tender. Remove from the heat. Allow to cool 10 minutes; place the fruit in the canning jars. Mix 2 cups of the peach liquid with the brandy. Simmer over low heat for 5 minutes. Pour the liquid over the fruit in the jars; seal. Ready to use in 4 days.

Yield: 10 8-ounce jars

Pickled Watermelon Rind

8¼ pounds watermelon rind

6 cups dark brown sugar

5 medium cinnamon sticks

16 cloves

6 whole allspice

4 cups vinegar

2 lemon rinds, grated

Remove the outermost part of the watermelon rind. Discard the outer-shell cuttings. Dice the remaining rind. Cover the diced rind with water in a large pot. Cook for 20 minutes over medium heat or until the rind is tender. Set in a cool, dry place for 12 hours.

In a saucepan, mix the sugar and spices with the vinegar. Boil for 5 minutes, stirring frequently. Drain the watermelon rind and add, with the grated lemon, to the sauce. Mix well. Pour into jars and seal.

Yield: 12 8-ounce jars

Sarah's Apple Chutney

2 pounds cooking apples,
   pared and quartered

2 cups apple cider vinegar

4 cups brown sugar

1½ lemons

2 small onions, diced

2 cups raisins

5 teaspoons ginger

1 teaspoon garlic powder

¾ teaspoon salt

¾ teaspoon mace

½ teaspoon red pepper

Place the apples in a large pot. Cover with the vinegar and sugar; mix well. Cook over medium-low heat until the apples are tender. Squeeze the lemon juice into the mixture. Grate the lemon rinds; add the rinds and other ingredients, stirring continuously. Bring to a boil. Reduce to low heat. Cover and simmer for 30 minutes. Allow the mixture to cool for 15 minutes. Pour into jars and seal.

Yield: 12 8-ounce jars

Pear Honey

8 cups ripe pears, peeled
and chopped very fine

5 cups sugar
1 cup crushed pineapple

Mix pears and sugar in large pot and boil 30 minutes. Then add 1 small can crushed pineapple and cook 15 minutes longer. Seal in jars.

Yield: 10 8-ounce jars

Fresh Fruit Honey Dressing

½ cup vinegar
¼ cup honey
¼ sugar
1 teaspoon dry mustard
dash of paprika

1 teaspoon celery seed
½ teaspoon celery salt
1 teaspoon onion juice
1 cup vegetable oil

Mix first five ingredients together. Boil three minutes and cool. Add rest of ingredients and shake or beat vigorously. Serve over fresh fruit. Refrigerate leftovers.

Yield: 2 cups

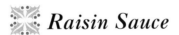 Raisin Sauce

2 cups water
1 cup raisins
1½ cups crushed pineapple
¼ cup pecan pieces, optional
½ cup brown sugar firmly packed
½ teaspoon ground cloves

½ teaspoon cinnamon
½ teaspoon dry mustard
½ teaspoon salt
1½ tablespoons cornstarch
1½ tablespoons vinegar
1½ tablespoons butter

To boiling water add raisins, pineapple and pecan pieces. Boil 5 minutes. Mix all dry ingredients and add to raisin-pineapple mixture. Add vinegar and butter. Stir often while cooking for 15 minutes.

Yield: 16 servings

Red Currant Sauce

1 10-ounce jar of currant jelly
2 tablespoons dry sherry

1 tablespoon soy sauce

Combine all ingredients in saucepan over medium-low heat. Simmer two minutes. Serve warm in separate pitcher.

Yield: 1¼ cups

Pickled Okra

6 garlic cloves
6 red hot peppers
40 to 50 small okra
6 teaspoons dill seed

1 quart vinegar
1 cup water
½ cup salt

Sterilize 6 pint jars. Place 1 garlic clove and 1 hot pepper in each jar. Pack firmly with okra. Add 1 teaspoon dill seed to each jar. Boil vinegar, water and salt. Simmer for 5 minutes and pour immediately over okra. Seal. Store in a cool, dark place and allow pickles to set for several weeks.

Note: Never use copper, brass or zinc utensils in canning. Use whole spices, not ground.

Desserts

Apple Crisp

APPLES	TOPPING
5 cups apples, peeled and sliced	½ cup rolled oats
2 tablespoons sugar	½ cup brown sugar
¼ teaspoon nutmeg	½ teaspoon cinnamon
½ teaspoon cinnamon	¼ cup butter or margarine
1 tablespoon fresh lemon juice	¼ cup flour

Gently toss apples with next four ingredients. Place apple mixture in the bottom of a 9x9x2-inch pan. Stir topping ingredients in a separate bowl until mixed thoroughly. Mixture will be crumbly. Sprinkle topping over apples evenly and gently press down. Bake at 375° about 30–35 minutes or until apples are bubbly and topping is lightly browned.

Yield: 8 servings

Apple Fritters

1 cup flour	½ cup brandy
¼ teaspoon salt	5 medium apples, pared
2½ tablespoons brown sugar	and cut into eighths
3 teaspoons butter, melted	2 cups shortening
2 eggs, separated	2 tablespoons sugar
⅔ cup whole milk	2½ tablespoons cinnamon

Sift together the flour and salt. Cream together the brown sugar and butter. Combine the flour and the egg whites, stiffly beaten. In a large bowl, mix together the creamed sugar and butter with the well-beaten egg yolks, milk and 3 teaspoons brandy. Add the dry ingredients; stir well until the batter is smooth. Soak the sliced apples in the brandy for 3 hours; drain and add the apples to the batter, mixing well.

Melt the shortening in a skillet at 325°. With a draining spoon, remove the apples from the batter and fry. Cook until the apples are a golden brown.

Combine the sugar and cinnamon; sprinkle over the apples and serve, topped with whipped cream.

Yield: 4 servings

114

Crispy Peach Cobbler

FROM THE ORDINARY

BATTER

1 tablespoon softened butter

¼ cup sugar

1 teaspoon vanilla

1 egg, beaten

½ cup flour

½ cup milk

3 cups sliced peaches

TOPPING

½ cup brown sugar

2 tablespoons melted butter

2 tablespoons sugar

2 tablespoons flour

1 cup oats

To make batter, cream butter and sugar with mixer in small bowl. Add remaining ingredients and mix well. Set aside. To make topping, mix all ingredients except oats. Add those last and stir until mixed. Butter 2-quart casserole. Pour in batter. Spoon peaches gently on top but do not stir. Sprinkle topping over mixture evenly. Bake at 350° for 45–60 minutes until topping begins to brown and batter is set.

Yield: 6–8 servings

Note: If using fresh peaches, peel, slice and simmer in saucepan over low heat until peaches are tender. You may add 1/4 cup sugar if peaches are not ripe.

Peach Cobbler

6 to 8 peaches

½ cup sugar

1 stick butter

¾ cup flour

2 teaspoons baking powder

¾ cup sugar

¾ cup milk

1 teaspoon vanilla

Peel and slice peaches. Place in saucepan and pour ½ cup sugar over fruit. Bring to a boil. Melt butter in deep ovenproof dish. Stir together flour, baking powder and sugar in separate bowl. Whisk in milk and vanilla. Pour flour mixture into butter. Do not stir. Pour fruit in middle of all of this. Again, do not stir. Bake at 350° for 45 minutes to 1 hour.

Virginia Apple Cake

2½ cups apples, peeled, cored and sliced

⅔ cup sugar

1 teaspoon cinnamon

1 lemon

1 tablespoon all-purpose flour

3 tablespoons melted butter

1 cup all-purpose flour

½ cup sugar

1 teaspoon double-acting
  baking powder

¼ teaspoon salt

2 egg yolks

1 tablespoon melted butter

¼ cup milk

Preheat oven to 425°. Grease a deep 8-inch pie pan and cover bottom well with apples. Sprinkle fruit with ⅔ cup sugar, cinnamon, grated rind and juice of the lemon. Dredge with 1 tablespoon flour and pour butter over surface. To prepare batter, sift together 1 cup flour, sugar, baking powder and salt. Beat and add egg yolks, 1 tablespoon butter and ¼ cup milk. Beat with swift strokes until blended. Cover fruit with batter. Bake cake for about 30 minutes. Reverse it on a platter. Cool slightly.

Banana Cake

2½ cups all-purpose flour

1¼ cups sugar

1½ teaspoons baking soda

1 teaspoon salt

1 teaspoon baking powder

½ cup butter, softened

½ cup buttermilk

1½ cups mashed ripe medium bananas

2 large eggs

⅔ cup walnuts, chopped

Preheat oven to 350°. Grease bottom and sides of 13 x 9 x 2-inch rectangular pan with shortening; lightly flour. Beat all ingredients except nuts in large bowl with electric mixer on low speed for 30 seconds, scraping bowl constantly. Beat on high speed 3 minutes, scraping bowl occasionally. Stir in nuts and pour into pan. Bake 45 to 50 minutes or until toothpick inserted in center comes out clean. Cool on wire rack.

Blackberry Jam Cake

1 cup butter

2 cups sugar

5 eggs

1 teaspoon soda

1 cup buttermilk

2 teaspoons cinnamon

2 teaspoons allspice

2 teaspoons cloves

2 teaspoons nutmeg

1 teaspoon salt

4 cups flour

2 teaspoons baking powder

1 cup blackberry jam

Cream butter and sugar well. Add eggs and beat well. Put soda in buttermilk. Sift spices in flour with baking powder (mix thoroughly). Add soda, buttermilk and dry ingredients alternately; beat well. Add jam last (fold in). Bake 1 hour at 300°. If desired, cover with caramel icing.

Garden Squash Cake

1 pound butternut squash

1 cup molasses

1 cup sugar

½ cup melted butter

3 cups flour

4 teaspoons baking powder

¼ teaspoon baking soda

½ cup milk

1 teaspoon vanilla extract

Boil the squash until tender; drain thoroughly and mash. Mix together the molasses, sugar and melted butter with 1 cup squash; beat until smooth and creamy. Sift together the flour, powder and soda; stir into the creamed mixture. Blend in the milk and vanilla extract. Pour the mix into a large greased loaf pan. Bake at 300° for 45 minutes or until done. Remove from the pan. Cool on a rack. When the cake has cooled, glaze with the following icing:

¾ cup confectioners sugar

2 teaspoons water

½ teaspoon vanilla extract

Mix the ingredients until well blended. Glaze.

Spice Nut Cake

½ cup shortening

1 cup sugar

2 cups of sifted flour

2 teaspoons baking powder

2 teaspoons cloves

2 teaspoons cinnamon

2 teaspoons allspice

½ teaspoon salt

½ cup milk

3 eggs

Cream shortening together, adding sugar gradually while beating. Measure and sift together the flour, baking powder, cloves, cinnamon, allspice and salt. Add to the sugar mixture alternately with the milk beating constantly. Last, fold in three egg whites beaten stiffly. Pour into a greased, floured, loaf-cake pan, and bake in 350° oven for 45 minutes.

Fresh Coconut Cake

1 cup butter

2 cups sugar

3½ cups flour

3½ teaspoons baking powder

1 cup milk

8 egg whites

½ teaspoon vanilla

½ teaspoon lemon extract

Cream butter, add sugar gradually. Cream well. Combine flour and baking powder and add to creamed mixture alternately with milk. Beat egg whites stiff but not dry. Add flavorings. Bake in 3 greased and floured 9-inch cake pans at 375° for about 30 to 35 minutes or until browned. Cool before icing.

Icing for Coconut Cake

3 cups granulated sugar

1 cup water

2 teaspoon vinegar

3 egg whites

½ teaspoon cream of tartar

1 teaspoon lemon extract

1 teaspoon vanilla

1½ cups freshly grated coconut

Stir together sugar, water and vinegar. Cook until it spins a fine thread. Beat egg whites with cream of tartar. Gradually add sugar mixture, beating constantly. Add lemon and vanilla extracts and mix well. Stir in coconut and spread on cooled cake layers.

Strawberry Shortcake

4 cups sliced strawberries

½ cup sugar, divided

2 cups flour

1 tablespoon baking powder

¼ teaspoon salt

½ cup butter

⅔ cup half-and-half

1 egg, beaten

2 cups sweetened whipped cream

Combine sliced strawberries and ¼ cup sugar; chill. Combine ¼ cup sugar, flour, baking powder, and salt. Cut in butter until mixture resembles coarse meal. Combine half-and-half and egg. Stir well, then add to flour mixture. Stir just until moistened. Spread mixture in a lightly-greased 8-inch square baking pan. Bake at 450° for 15 minutes or until golden brown. Cool 5 minutes, then turn out onto a wire rack.

Cut shortcake into 6 pieces. Slice each piece crosswise in half. Place bottom half of shortcake, cut side up, on a serving plate. Top with a dollop of whipped cream and 2½ tablespoons of strawberry mixture. Add second layer of shortcake, cut side down. Top with 2½ tablespoons of the strawberry mixture and a dollop of whipped cream. Repeat for remaining squares.

Yield: 6 servings

Kentucky Bourbon Cake

1½ cups butter or margarine

2¼ cups light brown sugar, packed

2 cups sugar

6 eggs

5½ cups sifted flour

¼ teaspoon salt

1 teaspoon mace

2 cups bourbon (bonded)

1 pound pecans, coarsely chopped

Cream butter; add half brown and white sugars. Beat until light and fluffy. In a separate bowl beat eggs and gradually add remaining sugars and continue to beat. Combine this with the butter mixture. Sift flour, salt and mace and fold into the egg-butter mixture alternately with the bourbon. Add pecans. Pour into well-greased 10-inch tube pan. Bake 350° for 1½ to 1¾ hours. Cool and turn out onto rack. This cake improves with age.

Old-Fashioned Fruit Cake

1 pound brown sugar

½ pound butter

5 eggs, separated

½ cup crushed pineapple

1 cup honey

½ cup strawberry preserves

½ pound Brazil nuts

1 cup black walnuts

½ pound English walnuts

½ pound almonds

½ pound figs

¼ pound crystallized pineapple

1 pound dates

2 cups raisins

¼ pound crystallized cherries

4 cups flour

2 teaspoons cinnamon

¼ teaspoon allspice

1 teaspoon baking powder

1 teaspoon baking soda

Cream sugar and butter; add egg yolks and cream together. Fold in juicy fruits, such as crushed pineapple, honey and preserves. Add chopped nuts and fruits which have been drenched in half of the flour. Fold in stiffly beaten egg white; add spices, baking powder and soda. Bake at 300° for about 4 hours. Put a pan of water under cake while baking.

Yield: 8½-pound cake

Susan's Pound Cake

1 cup butter

½ cup shortening

3 cups sugar

5 eggs

3 cups flour

1 teaspoon baking powder

½ teaspoon salt

2 tablespoons vanilla

1 cup milk

Cream butter, shortening and sugar. Add eggs one at a time, beating well after each addition. Sift flour with baking powder and salt. Add vanilla to milk. Add flour mixture alternately with the milk and mix well. Pour into greased and floured tube pan and bake at 350° for one hour and 10 minutes. Time may vary with ovens. To test doneness, insert toothpick until it comes out clean.

Yield: 24 servings

Chocolate Pound Cake

1 cup butter

½ cup vegetable shortening

3 cups sugar

5 eggs

1 teaspoon vanilla

3 cups flour, sifted

½ teaspoon baking powder

½ teaspoon salt

4 heaping tablespoons cocoa

1½ cups milk

Cream together butter and shortening. Add sugar and mix well. Add eggs one at a time, beating after each addition. Add vanilla. Combine dry ingredients and add alternately with milk to creamed mixture. Bake in greased 10-inch tube pan at 350° for 1 hour and 45 minutes (or about 80 minutes).

Deep, Dark Chocolate Cake

1¾ cups unsifted all-purpose flour

2 cups sugar

¾ cup cocoa

1½ teaspoons baking soda

1½ teaspoons baking powder

1 teaspoon salt

2 eggs

1 cup milk

½ cup vegetable oil

2 teaspoons vanilla

1 cup boiling water

Combine dry ingredients in large mixer bowl. Add remaining ingredients except boiling water; beat at medium speed 2 minutes. Stir in boiling water (batter will be thin.) Pour into two greased and floured 9-inch or three 8-inch layer pans or one 13 x 9 x 2-inch pan. Bake at 350° for 30 to 35 minutes for layers, 35 to 40 minutes for 13 x 9 x 2-inch pan, or until cake tester inserted in center comes out clean. Cool 10 minutes; remove from pans. Cool completely.

Chocolate Frosting with Cocoa

6 tablespoons butter or margarine
½ cup cocoa
2⅔ cups powdered sugar

4 to 5 tablespoons milk
1 tablespoon vanilla

Cream butter or margarine until softened in small mixer bowl. Add cocoa; blend well. Gradually add powdered sugar alternately with milk and vanilla; beat to spreading consistency. Spread frosting onto dessert with spatula.

Yield: 2 cups, enough to frost 2½ dozen cupcakes or an 8- to 9-inch layer cake.

Chocolate Satin Frosting

3½ 1-ounce squares
   unsweetened chocolate
3 cups sifted powdered sugar
4½ tablespoons hot water

1 egg
½ cup soft butter or margarine
1½ teaspoons vanilla

Melt chocolate in double boiler over hot water. Remove from heat. With mixer, blend in sugar and water. Beat in egg, then butter and vanilla. Frosting will be thin at this point, so place bowl in ice water; beat until spreading consistency.

Yield: Frosts tops and sides of two 9-inch layers

Frances Pattie's Caramel Icing

4 tablespoons butter

6 tablespoons milk or cream

1 cup brown sugar

2 cups powdered sugar

1 teaspoon vanilla

Melt butter. Add milk and brown sugar. Boil vigorously for 1 minute. Remove from heat. Add 1 cup powdered sugar and beat well. Cool slightly and add 1 teaspoon vanilla and 1 cup powdered sugar. Beat well. If too thick, add drops of milk or cream.

Yield: Frosts two 9-inch layers

Fluffy White Frosting

2 egg whites

¾ cups sugar

⅓ cup light corn syrup

2 tablespoons water

¼ teaspoon cream of tartar

¼ teaspoon salt

1 teaspoon vanilla

Put first 5 ingredients in top of double boiler, over boiling water. Beat with hand beater around 7 minutes or with electric beater 4 minutes or until mixture stands in peaks. Remove from heat and set in cold water and add vanilla. Continue beating until icing stands in shiny peaks stiff enough to hold shape. Spread on cake immediately.

Yield: Frosts two 9-inch layers

Gentlemen's Favorite Cake Topping

3 large firm apples

1 cup sugar

1 egg, beaten

2 teaspoons lemon juice

Peel apples and grate. Add sugar and stir. Add egg and cook in saucepan over medium heat. Stir constantly until egg sets. Add lemon juice and blend. While warm, spread on baked cake.

Yield: Frosts one 9-inch layer

Flaky Pastry

2 cups flour

3 teaspoons sugar

¾ teaspoon salt

⅔ cup shortening

5 tablespoons cold water

Combine the dry ingredients in a large bowl. Blend in the shortening and water. Work the pastry, using additional cold water if necessary. Wrap the dough in wax paper. Store in the refrigerator for 5 hours before using.

Note: For a pre-baked shell, bake the pie crust at 400° for 15 to 17 minutes.

Yield: 1 pie crust

Katie Lou's Southern Pecan Pie

3 eggs

¾ cup granulated sugar

1 cup dark corn syrup

1 teaspoon vanilla

¼ cup melted butter or margarine

1 cup pecans, broken in pieces

Pinch of salt

Unbaked pie shell

Beat eggs. Add sugar and beat well. Stir in syrup, vanilla and butter. Add pecans. Pour into unbaked pie shell. Bake at 450° for ten minutes. Lower temperature to 300° and bake for 35 minutes. If pie doesn't seem set, cook five minutes longer.

Yield: 8 servings

Katie Lou's Chess Pie

4 eggs

2 cups sugar

2 tablespoons cornmeal

5 tablespoons buttermilk

1 stick margarine

2 teaspoons vanilla

Pinch of salt

Unbaked pie shell

Mix together and pour into unbaked pie shell. Bake at 415° for 15 minutes. Reduce heat to 315° and continue baking for 45 minutes.

Yield: 6 servings

Elizabeth Stargell's Lemon Chess Pie

½ cup melted butter

1¾ cups sugar

2 tablespoons flour

4 eggs, well beaten

3 lemons, juice and grated rind

Pinch of salt

Unbaked pie shell

Combine ingredients and pour into a deep dish pie crust. Bake at 350° for 1 hour or until golden brown.

Yield: 8 servings

Southern Fudge Pie

½ cup butter or margarine

2 squares unsweetened chocolate

¼ cup flour

2 eggs

1 cup sugar

Dash salt

1¼ teaspoons vanilla extract

Unbaked pie shell

Over low heat, melt the butter and chocolate. Mix the flour, eggs and sugar. Add this mixture with the salt and vanilla to the chocolate-butter sauce. Pour into a pie shell. Bake at 350° for 30 minutes or until firm to the touch. Serve with scoops of vanilla ice cream and/or whipped cream.

Yield: 6 servings

Black Bottom Pie

1 tablespoon gelatin
¼ cup cold water
¾ cup sugar, divided
4 teaspoons cornstarch
4 eggs, separated
2 cups scalded milk
1½ ounces melted unsweetemed chocolate

1 teaspoon vanilla
1 tablespoon rum
¼ teaspoon cream of tartar
½ ounce grated semisweet chocolate
Baked pie shell or baked crumb crust

Soak gelatin in cold water. Combine sugar and cornstarch. Beat egg yolks until light and slowly stir milk into eggs. Stir in sugar mixture. Cook in the top of a double boiler, stirring often, about 20 minutes or until custard heavily coats the spoon. Take 1 cup of the custard and add melted chocolate. Beat until well blended. Cool, add vanilla and pour into the crust. Dissolve soaked gelatin in remaining hot custard. Let it cool, but not set. Stir in rum. Beat 3 egg whites until blended. Add cream of tartar and beat until peaks form. Gradually add ¼ cup sugar. Fold egg whites into custard. Cover chocolate custard with rum-flavored custard. Top with grated chocolate and chill to set.

Yield: 8 servings

Shoo-Fly Pie

½ stick butter
1 cup dark brown sugar
1½ cups all-purpose flour
¾ teaspoon baking soda
⅔ cup molasses
⅔ cup boiling water

½ teaspoon cinnamon
½ teaspoon cloves
½ teaspoon ginger
Dash nutmeg
Dash of salt

Cream together the butter and sugar. Blend in the flour. Grease an 8 x 8-inch pan. Pat down a layer of the crumbled mixture. In another bowl, combine the remaining ingredients until creamy. Cover the crust with a layer of the liquid filling. Repeat the layering until all of the ingredients are gone and there is a crust on top. Bake at 350° for 40 to 50 minutes or until golden brown. Serve warm.

Yield: 8 servings

Traditional Pumpkin Pie

2 cups boiled pumpkin,
   mashed and strained
2 eggs, well-beaten
1½ cups whole milk
5½ teaspoons molasses

⅔ cup dark brown sugar
¼ cup brandy
1 teaspoon salt
1¼ teaspoons cinnamon
1¼ teaspoons cloves

Mix all of the ingredients together until well-blended. Pour the mix into an unbaked pie shell. Bake at 375° for 1 hour or until done.

Yield: 8 servings

Southern Sweet Potato Pie

3 egg yolks
¾ cup sugar
4 tablespoons butter
1 cup mashed sweet potatoes

1½ cups milk
⅓ teaspoon grated nutmeg
3 egg whites
1 unbaked pie shell

Beat egg yolks, add sugar, butter, mashed sweet potatoes and milk. Mixture should be thin. Add flavoring. Beat egg whites until stiff and fold into the sweet potato mixture. Pour into unbaked pastry shell and bake in a 450° oven for 10 minutes. Reduce heat to 350° and bake about 35 minutes longer or until custard is set. Knife inserted into mixture should come out clean.

Yield: 6 servings

Chocolate Pudding ca. 1894

4 tablespoons cornstarch	2½ tablespoons cocoa
4 cups milk	3 tablespoons sugar

Warm 1 cup of milk in double boiler. Dissolve cornstarch. Before it thickens, add the cocoa and whisk to dissolve. Add sugar. Mix in rest of milk and stir until pudding coats the back of a wooden spoon, about 8–10 minutes over medium heat. Pour into bowls and refrigerate until set. Serve with whipped cream.

Yield: 6 servings

Baked Custard

4 cups whole milk	⅛ teaspoon salt
1 cup sugar	1 teaspoon vanilla or scraped
4 whole eggs	seeds from 1-inch length of
	vanilla bean

Blend milk, sugar, eggs and salt. Beat well, add vanilla and stir to mix. Pour into baking dish or individual cups. Place dish or cups into pan of hot water. Bake at 300° for one hour or more in the dish or 20 to 30 minutes in individual cups until custard is set. Chill before serving.

Yield: 10 servings

The Michie's Christmas Bread

2 cups flour
1 cup milk
3 tablespoons butter

1 teaspoon salt
1 teaspoon baking powder
1 teaspoon baking soda

Mix the ingredients together and roll out ½-inch thick on a floured board. Cut with a biscuit cutter and then bake at 350° for 7 minutes. Allow biscuits to cool and then top the biscuits with the following icing:

¾ cup walnuts, chopped
½ cup candied red or
    green cherries, chopped
½ cup confectioners sugar

½ cup milk
¼ cup raisins
½ teaspoon lemon extract

Combine the ingredients; mix well. When the biscuits have sufficiently cooled, top with the icing.

Yield: 9 servings

Bread Pudding

4 eggs
4 cups milk
2 cups bread, broken
½ cup sugar

1 tablespoon butter
Nutmeg
4 tablespoons sugar for egg whites
Damson preserves

Separate eggs and put whites in refrigerator. Warm milk over low heat and add bread, sugar, butter and egg yolks. When mixture becomes warm, pour into shallow, greased baking dish (2-quart). Sprinkle with nutmeg. Bake 20 to 30 minutes in a 350° oven or until firm. Cool. Add pinch of salt to egg whites beating until soft peak and then gradually add sugar 1 tablespoon at a time. Cover top of pudding, first with a layer of Damson preserves and then with the egg whites. Put in a 425° oven until brown, about 3 minutes.

Yield: 6 servings

Mrs. Brooks' Bread Pudding with Whipped Cream

8 slices bread, cubed

2 cups warm milk

2 eggs, separated

¼ teaspoon salt

4 tablespoons sugar, divided

¾ teaspoon vanilla extract

3 cups whipping cream

Spread the bread cubes in a baking dish; let stand for 1 hour uncovered. Pour the milk over the bread; cover and allow the bread to absorb the milk. Add the egg yolks with the salt, sugar and vanilla. Add the two egg whites, stiffly beaten. Stir the entire mixture. Bake at 350° for 50 to 60 minutes.

Topping:

Blend 3 cups whipping cream and 3 tablespoons sugar in a bowl until peaks form. When the pudding has cooled, cut into squares, top with whipped cream and serve.

Yield: 6 to 8 servings

Great-Grandmother's Gingerbread Recipe

½ cup butter and lard mixed

½ cup sugar

1 egg

1 cup molasses

1½ teaspoons soda

2½ cups sifted flour

½ teaspoon salt

1 teaspoon cinnamon

½ teaspoon cloves

1 cup hot water

Cream shortening and sugar. Add beaten egg, molasses, then dry ingredients which have been sifted together. Add hot water last and beat until smooth. Bake in greased shallow pan at 350° for 40 to 45 minutes.

Yield: 15 slices

Town Crier's Gingerbread Cookies

1 cup shortening	1½ teaspoons baking soda
1 cup sugar	1 teaspoon ginger
2 tablespoons vinegar	1 teaspoon cinnamon
1 egg	½ teaspoon cloves
1 cup molasses	½ teaspoon salt
5 cups flour	

Cream the shortening and sugar then add the vinegar and egg, beating well. Stir in molasses. Sift together the flour, soda and spices. Combine the two mixtures, blending well. Knead the dough for 5 minutes. Separate the dough into two balls. Wrap each in wax paper and refrigerate for 4 hours.

On a floured board, roll out a ball of dough ⅛ to ¼-inch thickness. Cut in desired shapes with cookie cutters. Place 1 inch apart on a greased cookie sheet. Bake at 375° for 7 minutes. Cool slightly, then remove from the cookie sheet and place on a rack.

Yield: 8 dozen

Ginger Cookies

1½ cups butter or margarine	4 teaspoons soda
2 cups sugar	2 teaspoons cinnamon
½ cup molasses	1 teaspoon ginger
2 eggs	1 teaspoon cloves
4 cups flour	Sugar

Melt butter. Add sugar, molasses and eggs to butter. Beat well. Sift flour, soda and spices. Add this mixture to make a dough. Refrigerate for several hours. Roll into small balls. Roll in sugar and bake at 350° for 8 to 10 minutes.

Yield: 6 dozen

Little Lizzies
(Bite-sized fruit cakes)

¼ cup margarine or butter	1½ teaspoons cinnamon
½ cup light brown sugar	2¾ cups white raisins
2 eggs	½ cup bourbon
1½ cups flour	4 cups pecans, chopped
1½ teaspoons baking soda	2¾ cups candied cherries, chopped
½ teaspoon cloves	1¼ cups citron
½ teaspoon nutmeg	1¼ cups pineapple

Soak the raisins in bourbon overnight. Cream the margarine or butter with the sugar; add the eggs and beat well. Sift together the flour, baking soda and spices. Add the raisins, nuts and fruits; mix together. Combine all of the mixture together in a large bowl. Drop on greased cookie sheets. Bake at 325° for 15 minutes.

Yield: 8 dozen

Wine Jelly

3 envelopes unflavored gelatin	Frosted grapes
1½ cups cold water	Mint sprigs
1½ cups sugar	Whipped cream
½ cup lemon juice	Brandy, optional
3 cups red wine	

Sprinkle gelatin over water in medium saucepan. Place over low heat; stir constantly until gelatin dissolves, about 5 minutes. Remove from heat, add sugar and stir until dissolved. Stir in lemon juice and wine. Pour into shallow 6 cup mold. Chill until firm. Unmold, garnish with frosted grapes and mint sprigs. Serve with whipped cream with dash of brandy folded in. Frosted grapes are made by dipping small clusters of the fruit into slightly beaten egg whites and sprinkling with granulated sugar. Place on waxed paper and let stand to dry.

Yield: 8–10 servings

Raisin Cookies

2½ cups raisins
1 cup boiling water
1 teaspoon baking soda
1 cup butter or margarine
2 cups sugar
3 beaten eggs
1 teaspoon vanilla extract

1 teaspoon lemon or orange extract
4 cups flour
1½ teaspoons baking powder
1 teaspoon cinnamon
½ teaspoon salt
½ teaspoon allspice

Boil the raisins in the water for 7 minutes. Stir in the baking soda; allow the ingredients to cool. Melt the butter or margarine; cream with the sugar, eggs and extracts. Mix all with the cooling raisins. Sift the flour, baking powder, cinnamon, salt and allspice together and add to the raisin mixture. Mix well. Drop the dough from a spoon onto a greased cookie sheet, about 1½ to 2 inches apart. Bake at 400° until browned, about 12 to 15 minutes. Let the cookies cool on racks.

Yield: 6 dozen

Springhouse Christmas Cookies

½ cup sugar
½ cup shortening
1 egg yolk
1 tablespoon milk
2 teaspoons vanilla extract

1½ cups enriched flour
½ teaspoon baking powder
½ teaspoon salt
½ cup red colored sugar
½ cup green colored sugar

Cream the white sugar and shortening; stir in the egg yolk, milk and vanilla until well-blended. Sift together the flour, powder and salt; add to the creamed mixture. Knead the mix for 3 minutes. Divide the dough into halves. Roll the dough up and wrap in wax paper. Chill for 2½ hours.

Slice the dough thin. Put the colored sugar in shallow dishes. Press the slices of dough into the desired colored sugar. Place on a greased cookie sheet with the sugar side face-up. Bake at 375° for 8 to 10 minutes.

Yield: 4 to 6 dozen

Maple Syrup Shortbread

Shortbread:

½ cup (1 stick) unsalted butter, room temperature

¼ cup sugar

1 cup all-purpose flour

Maple topping:

¾ cup brown sugar

⅓ cup pure maple syrup

1 tablespoon unsalted butter

1 egg

1 teaspoon vanilla

½ cup chopped toasted walnuts

For shortbread: Generously butter 9-inch square baking dish. Cream butter and sugar until light and fluffy. Add flour and mix just until blended. Do not form ball. Pat into bottom of prepared dish. Bake at 350° until shortbread is light brown, about 25 minutes.

For topping: Beat sugar, maple syrup and butter to blend. Beat in egg and vanilla. Pour over shortbread. Sprinkle evenly with walnuts. Bake at 350° until topping is set, about 25 minutes. Cool on rack. Cut into 1½-inch squares. Store in airtight container.

Scottish Shortbread

1 cup butter, softened

½ cup fine granulated sugar

2 cups flour

Cream together butter and sugar until light and fluffy. Gradually add flour. Beat about 5 minutes until smooth. Spread evenly in ungreased 9 x 13-inch pan. Bake at 300° for 30 to 40 minutes until lightly browned. After removing from oven, prick all over with fork and cut into bars. Cool completely.

Yield: 4 dozen.

Ambrosia

8 to 12 oranges peeled and sections removed

1 pineapple, diced

1¼ cups grated coconut

Powdered sugar, to taste

3 tablespoons orange juice

Place a layer of oranges in dish then pineapple, then coconut. Sprinkle powdered sugar over all. Repeat and end with sugar. Pour orange juice over all. Cover and refrigerate.

Yield: 10 to 12 servings

Persimmon Pudding

2 cups persimmon pulp

3 beaten eggs

1½ cups sugar

1½ cups flour

1 teaspoon baking soda

1 teaspoon baking powder

½ teaspoon salt

¾ cup milk

½ teaspoon cinnamon

½ teaspoon allspice

1 teaspoon vanilla

To prepare pulp, select and wash ripe persimmons. Remove skins and seeds and mash well. Add small amount of water if necessary and put through colander. Measure 2 cups of pulp and add remaining ingredients. Mix well. Pour into buttered casserole dish. Bake at 350° for 1 hour. To serve, cut into squares and top with whipped cream.

Yield: 8 to 10 servings

Colonial Syllabub

4 cups whipping cream	1 cup sherry
¾ cup sugar	½ cup brandy
¾ cup lemon juice	nutmeg for garnish

Whip the cream until it forms peaks. Add sugar and mix until it dissolves. When cream is stiff, add lemon juice, sherry and brandy. Whip for about two minutes longer. Spoon into parfait glasses and refrigerate for 3 to 4 days. The dessert separates after a couple of days with cream on top and liquid at bottom of glass.

Yield: 6 to 8 servings

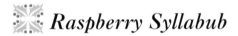 Raspberry Syllabub

4 cups whipping cream	1 cup semi-dry white wine
¾ cup sugar	1 pint fresh raspberries
1 cup Chambord liqueur	1 bunch mint leaves

Whip the cream until it forms peaks. Add sugar and mix until it dissolves. When cream is stiff, add Chambord and white wine. Whip for about two minutes longer. Spoon into parfait glasses and refrigerate for 3 to 4 days. Before serving, garnish with raspberries and mint sprigs.

Yield: 6 to 8 servings

Note: Syllabub was a favorite early American drink and was sipped through the foam on the top. At Michie Tavern, we serve syllabub at our Yuletide dinners as a dessert that is eaten with a spoon. The best spoonful is the last as the liquor settles to the bottom.

History of Michie Tavern

Facts and legends have seemingly been partners with every historical site; thus, the following pages have been written with due respect to history, but also include many of the legends that are a part of Michie's Tavern.

The Proprietor

Corporal William Michie was at Valley Forge when he received an urgent message to return home. Leaving behind the winter encampment, Michie commenced the tedious journey to Virginia only to learn upon his arrival that his ailing father had passed on.

The year was 1777 and it was a time for change, rebuilding and reorganizing in young William's life. His father, "Scotch" John, had bequeathed a large parcel of land which William had developed earlier with his father's permission. This site was the original 1735 land grant to Major John Henry, father of our famous orator Patrick Henry. John Michie had purchased this tract in 1746 and within ten years bought the rest of Maj. Henry's holdings in Albemarle County. The Blue Ridge Mountains surrounded this region and, because it was so highly populated with deer, the area was dubbed Buck Mountain. A creek by the same name was less than one mile away, and the fields were ideal for the cultivation of wheat and tobacco. The property was fed by a natural spring, and here William settled into a small, but sturdy, cabin by the side of the road.

138

Had William believed he would be living a solitary, isolated life, he was mistaken. The Buck Mountain Road led to the county courthouse and soon became a popular stagecoach route. In addition, taverns were a scarcity and roads were of a crude nature—often mere Indian paths. A ten-mile journey often constituted a full day's travel. A visitor to Virginia in the early 1700s wrote, "I traveled till noon without food in great heat through the wilderness, but did not meet a single person, the road becoming smaller and smaller…I was alone and lost in this wild place." William's cabin was a welcome site to weary travelers who often knocked on his door requesting food and shelter for the night. "Strangers," as travelers were called in the 18th century, were welcomed, and it was not uncommon for William to offer his own berth for tired guests. Even the mattress of cornhusks or straw pallets by the hearth were welcomed respites from the road. Hospitality was extended with few hardships, for William simply shared the food and accommodations available to him and enjoyed the diverse company and news from distant lands.

Original section of Michie Tavern ca. 1784

Michie's Tavern had numerous outbuildings.

Inn: The Beginning

When visits by Strangers became more frequent, William decided to open
his doors as a tavern. He hired an itinerant carpenter to build a large,
commodious dwelling several yards from his home. The carpenter received
precise plans on constructing Michie's three-story Inn. The Tavern would
have a large foyer, and to the eastern side there would be a parlor for
gentlemen. Here gentry could sleep or partake in occasional gaming. On the
opposite side of the hall would be a chamber for female travelers. This room,
William instructed, would be more elaborate in decor, and the carpenter
should pay special attention to a detailed design in the wooden mantle and
wall moldings. The upstairs Long Room or Ballroom would also be more
elaborate, and above this room ample attic space would serve as an additional sleeping area on crowded nights. The Keeping Hall downstairs would
feature a large brick hearth where food could be kept warm after it was
prepared in the Log Kitchen, the closest outbuilding to the Inn. The
Kitchen was very important to innkeepers because the largest percentage of

their income was derived from the sale of meals. Typical dishes prepared in this log structure would be ham, bacon, fish, fowl, dried venison, Indian or wheaten bread, and eggs. Milk and cheese would be kept in the Spring House adjacent to the Kitchen. The other service buildings would include a smoke house, well, outhouse or "necessary," and barn.

Townspeople often considered country inns as the poorer sisters of city taverns, but William felt confident that once his building was completed his Tavern would rival the most elaborate accommodations in town. In addition, William had the land which afforded the opportunity to place a gentlemanly bet on a good horse race or cockfight. William also believed that taverns located on the outskirts of town were more serviceable to travelers in want of necessary refreshment. Often, isolated taverns, which were initially established for travelers, later became the nucleus of settlements and centers of communication for clientele. Michie's Tavern would later serve as a post office and makeshift school. The Ballroom became a place for Sunday worship until the Buck Mountain Church was constructed.

Drinking was the most popular pastime in the 18th century.

141

The Tavern Rules

William was not one to refuse an occasional rum punch or game of cards. However, as a magistrate, vestryman and sheriff, he was accustomed to regulations. Soon after he set out his Tavern sign and opened his doors as an Inn, he posted the Tavern rules and fees. These fees were not always paid through monetary exchange. As was the custom in the 18th century, nearly two-thirds of all financial transactions were through barter while the other third was in cash. The Tavern proprietor most likely received furnishings from a cabinetmaker or shoes from a shoemaker in exchange for rum. A person could purchase almost two quarts of rum in exchange for a day's labor. Transactions were recorded in Michie's daybook as they occurred and were later transferred into his ledger each night before he retired.

Another rule, *No More Than Four to Sleep in One Bed*, raised few eyebrows. In fact, failure to share one's bed with a stranger might label a man as "unfriendly" or unreasonably "fastidious." Sleeping was not the private act it is today, and guests merely rented a space to sleep. Although a traveler might awaken to a bed full of strangers, there were benefits to this practice. Two or more travelers generating heat during the cold winter months was

The seasons dictated which foods to prepare.

142

The innkeeper set aside a special room for female travelers.

practical. Taverns usually offered beds in each room, and tucked beneath these high rope beds were trundle bedsteads which would be brought out at night. Mattresses or straw pallets were also available on crowded evenings.

Patrons probably grumbled about Michie's rule, *No Boots to be Worn in Bed*. A good pair of boots was expensive. A traveler feared that if he removed his boots at night they would be gone by morning. However, linens were equally expensive, and few innkeepers could afford a surplus of bedding.

Before the kitchen was amply governed by such help as Suey, Bet, Mary and Violet, the servants were known to imbibe their favorite refreshment or help themselves to meals when carrying such to the Keeping Hall from the Kitchen. Therefore, William added to his list of rules, *No Beer Allowed in the Kitchen*. Legend proclaims that he also ordered the servants to sing each time they brought meals to the Inn so that none of the food could be devoured.

Tinkers and Razor Grinders were not taken in. These itinerant handy-men were not considered the social equals of Mr. Michie's other guests and had the reputation of being thieves. Tavern proprietors were also prohibited by law from entertaining blacks, apprentices, Indians, servants and even seamen, unless they had permission from their captains or masters.

143

Tavern Prospers

In 1784 William petitioned to operate an Ordinary in his home. Because of the new government, a license was now required. Under British rule, such was never obtained or deemed necessary. By this time the Tavern was a popular stopping place for villagers as well as travelers and during "Public Times" or elections at the courthouse nearby, the Inn was filled to capacity. Seeing the need for expansion, William added a hyphen between the existing Tavern and his adjacent

Perishables were kept fresh and cool in the spring house.

cabin. Once these two structures were connected, the Inn offered two extra sleeping areas plus a Tap Bar near the far end of the Gentlemen's Parlor. No doubt this bar became the most frequented area of the Inn where spirits were dispensed to the gentry from the inside or to the coachmen on the porch through a small shutter-like window. The bar was also the most likely spot to post news from the Virginia House of Burgesses. William was a politically active man, and a crowded Inn afforded the opportunity to express his views. Earlier in 1779, when local countrymen were weakening in their support of America's cause, William signed the Albemarle Declaration of Independence and most likely persuaded his patrons to follow suit. One can almost imagine the heated political discussions that took place before a Tavern hearth or over a tankard of ale or spiced rum.

But even with such outstanding prosperity, William could see the need for greater self sufficiency and further expansion. Lack of capital, however, was one of the main obstacles standing in his way of achieving this goal.

As time passed and funds were finally accrued, he chose a lot not far from the Tavern, and with craftsmen employed, he began constructing a grist mill. Grist mills were sparsely located, especially in the Southern colonies. For a number of years William had spent many a day riding to the closest mill to sell his grain or buy the necessary flour. Once the mill was completed it would benefit not only himself but local farmers as well because the distance to be traveled in most instances would be lessened considerably. Years later, not far from the mill, the Michies constructed a General Store. They named it Longwood and operated it successfully for many years.

Ghosts

In 1811 William Michie died leaving the Tavern to his son, William Jr. The Tavern-plantation stayed in the Michie family until 1910. Records indicate that the homestead was used as a place of business up until the 1850s.

In the wake of new highways being established, the old Buck Mountain Road soon fell into disuse. A sparse number of the local populace can remember attending festivities at the Tavern about the turn of the century, but as time went on visitors sharply declined. The doors were eventually closed and the old Inn soon became the focal point of ghost stories.

A tale that has persisted through the years describes a fatigued wayfarer stopping in front of the Tavern one night to rest for awhile. When he heard the sounds of gurgling water he walked around the premises searching for a well or spring nearby. Upon finding the well, he saw someone before him drinking water by the bucketful. On his remarking at the stranger's abnormal thirst, the drinker answered that when one has been in hell as long as he, he'd be thirsty too.

Stories ran amuck, each one being spiced a little bit more, when told amongst friends. It has been said that the spirit of Scotch John pounds out nails and horseshoes from iron during the dark of the night. No one has ever seen the ghost, but many a farmer has claimed to have found newly-made articles such as these, strewn about the property upon inspection the next day.

It has also been said that a woman could often be heard sobbing and moaning while searching for her lost child. This woman was a servant when William ran the Inn. Apparently, one of her children had eaten a tomato that was considered the poisonous fruit of the Devil and commonly called "The Devil's Apple." The other servants were afraid of this youngster who now possessed magic powers. That night the child disappeared. Some descendants of the family claim that the eldest slave did away with the child to protect the others from harm. Still, others believe that the child fled to the North.

Another yarn narrated is that nightfall often left the servants ill at ease, as so many were said to have seen ghosts running about the homestead. Some of the servants believed that the old hoot owl who nestled in the trees was actually the ghost of John Michie. Legends speak of Scotch John hooting occasionally at his son, when William acted without his belated father's approval.

Past Preserved

In 1927 a local businesswoman, Mrs. Mark Henderson, expressed an interest in purchasing Michie Tavern. It was remotely located and rapidly deteriorating, but she felt confident that it was the ideal structure in which to house her vast collection of antiques and open a museum. An astute entrepreneur, Mrs. Henderson had paid special attention to a new and growing industry in our nation. The rise in automobile production and ownership, coupled with the drop in workweek hours and higher wages,

The keeping room was a hub of activity.

spurred the development of tourism. In addition, she closely watched the growth of a new movement taking hold in our country and soon found herself a pioneer in these preservation activities. Monticello had been opened for several years and was drawing thousands of visitors. Mrs. Henderson was merely following the precepts of her preservation peers when she decided to move Michie Tavern to a more accessible location. What better site than at the foot of Carter's Mountain, one-half mile from Jefferson's home. Within three months the old Inn had been painstakingly numbered, dismantled, and moved 17 miles by horse and wagon and truck to its new location. Little did Mrs. Henderson know, the move itself would become a historic event, and her efforts would ultimately lead to Michie Tavern's designation as a Virginia Historic Landmark. Michie Tavern opened as a museum in 1928. As in its heyday, the Tavern was once again located on a busy thoroughfare and welcoming Strangers at its door.

Today the Meadow Run Gristmill houses the General Store.

History of Meadow Run Mill

Approximately two hundred years have passed since the Michies operated a mill. Unfortunately, the mill fell from decay, its timbers having suffered from dry rot. But in order to keep tradition alive, as well as recreate the effect of 18th-century life, Michie Tavern relocated another mill to its grounds. The Meadow Run Mill, once located at Laurel Hill, Virginia, has been reconstructed piece by piece, and its appearance resembles that of the mill established by the Michies. The General Store, housed in the Meadow Run Mill, depicts the mercantile atmosphere of Longwood, the store the Michies used to run.

The factual history of the Meadow Run Mill remains vague. The first claims of its existence come from the ancestry of the Coiners, whose homestead was located in Crimora during the 1750s. The ancestors spoke of two mills being in operation at that time. One of these mills, located on Christians Creek, was destroyed by fire several years ago. The other mill was located on Meadow Run.

It is believed that the plans for the mill were drawn up in 1764, and that the actual construction began in 1770 when the site for the mill was cleared,

148

and the mortar for the foundation was being prepared. Even though the construction of the mill was incomplete, legend has it that this site was used as a military depot where armaments were stored during the Revolutionary period.

Legend also tells of the mill beginning as a coffin factory, the construction of the mill having been concluded prior to 1797. The actual owner and operator of the mill at that time remains somewhat of a mystery. It has been said that the owner of the coffin factory would pluck a "horse reed" from the banks of Meadow Run and then travel to the home of the newly deceased to measure the length of the body. Returning to the factory, he would take the reed, which he had cut to the exact length, and use such to determine the size of the coffin. Once the reed was used, the coffin maker would place it in front of a window facing the road.

Quite often, local townspeople riding by on the way to the market place would see the reed in the window, thus stopping to inquire of the deceased. Upon arrival at the market place, the villagers would then spread the news of the death.

Another story which echoes from the past tells of possible tragedy and certainly creates an atmosphere of mystery. During the early 1800s the owner of the mill had a lovely fair-haired daughter, who was very much in love with a young apprentice miller. The girl's father, however, did not approve of the young man. Consequently, the lovers began to meet secretly, primarily at night. The lovely maiden, standing on the balcony over the wheel of the mill would flash a coin in the light of the night, signaling to her true love that her father was asleep. At the other side of the stream the apprentice would flash a similar coin in acknowledgment. The lover would then cross the stream to the wheel. The young man's sweetheart, on the balcony above, would lock the turning wheel by wedging a piece of timber between the hub and the mill wall. Once the nave ceased turning, the girl's lover would climb up the wheel onto the balcony. This romance carried on for some time, until one night the wedge of wood slipped from its place, unlocking the massive wheel. Because of the man's weight, the wheel began to turn very quickly. The maiden, in her terror, hoped to save his life by leaning over the balcony and grasping his hand. In doing so, she was torn from her stance over the railing of the balcony. The following day, coins were seen glistening from the stream in the early morning sun.

It is believed by some people that the lovers perished, having been washed downstream, never to be found. Others claim the young couple ran off to spend their lives together. However, to this day it is said that during the light of the moon, one may still see the flashing of coins and hear the calls of the lovers.

Water powered this 18th century gristmill.

As well as being a site for grinding operations, the mill also served as a gathering place for area residents. Some of these gatherings were for quilting or canning; the women would meet with their sewing or produce and make fine quilts stuffed with goose down, or make jams and preserves. Local fiddlers, harmonizing with banjo and guitar players, would provide lively music for these and other festivities.

An elderly gent once spoke of whiskey being made in a distillery set up at the mill. Though proof was lacking, he emphatically said that some kind of drink was needed to entertain friends and that, with corn and rye being so readily available, "moonshine" was bound to be one of the miller's products.

Between 1821 and 1855, the mill was sold several times. In 1856, Windle and Mary Sites purchased this property and continued running the milling operations. It is believed that the Sites, who owned the mill during the Civil War, were most pleasant and kind in nature. Windle was a great sympathizer of the slaves' predicament and their quest for freedom. So too were he and his wife pacifists by way of their religious beliefs. When Yankee troops came to burn the mill down, Sites convinced the commanding officer that the slaves were free. The leader of the troops, having spoken to the slaves regarding the miller's claims, and having found such claims to be true, decided to spare the mill. As time passed, the officer made an agreement with Windle Sites by which the mill would be used as an interim type of hospital. Soon after the agreement was made, the Yankee soldiers commenced bringing their wounded to the mill, placing the casualties into the wheat bins on the upper floor.

Approximately three decades later, during the autumn of 1888, Windle Sites sold the mill. After changing hands a few more times, the mill was purchased by John Drumheller in 1896. His son, Carson Drumheller, was the last person to run the mill, keeping the operation intact until 1958. In 1974, the Meadow Run Mill was procured by Michie Tavern for the purpose of restoring and preserving this unusual aspect of American heritage.

Present Day Michie Tavern

Interactive Tours
18th-century lifestyles become a sensory experience where one engages the past to provide everlasting memories. Once you cross the threshold to Old Michie Tavern, you are removed from the 21st-century and will experience the life of travelers during the late 1700s. The tour is educational, fun and appropriate for adults and youth alike.

Lively Activities
Dance a colonial reel, write with a quill pen or slake your thirst with a tankard punch. Try to play a period musical instrument and fill the room with the dulcimer's sweet notes.

Especially for Youth
Our young adventurers hone their skills of discovery by participating in Mr. Michie's Treasure Hunt. Unravel the innkeeper's clues to the past and be rewarded with a bag of (chocolate) gold coins. Don period apparel or play 18th-century games. Let us custom-design a tour for your group.

Shopping
Located behind the Tavern in the Sowell House, **The Clothier** features period apparel, quilts and accessories.

The Tavern Gift Shop is adjacent to The Ordinary and offers a wide selection of historical reproductions and an attractive line of gifts, which reflect the original Tavern.

Housed within the Grist Mill, **The General Store** offers shopping in an old mercantile atmosphere. Two floors abound with gifts, collectibles, pewter, jewelry, books, vintage coins, Virginia's Finest foods and wines, and a huge selection of old-fashioned candy.

Index

Mail Order

Michie Tavern offers a variety of private label mixes. Tavern Midday Fare staples, such as our chicken breader, duplicate the ingredients prepared by our chefs. These mixes offer distinct flavors, which are reminiscent of old-fashioned recipes lovingly prepared and baked by hand.

Tavern Chicken Breader

Buttermilk Biscuit Mix

Cornbread Mix

Stone Ground Self-rising
   White Cornmeal

Stone Ground
   Whole Wheat Flour

Garlic & Herb Bread Mix

18th Century Spoon Bread Mix

Stone Ground White Grits

Old Mill Pancake & Waffle Mix

Sweet Potato Scone Mix

Lemon Blueberry Scone Mix

Cinnamon Muffin Mix

Old Virginia Pound Cake Mix

Fruit Cobbler Mix

Scottish Shortbread Mix

Ginger & Spice Cookie Mix

Brownie Mix

Inquire about Michie Tavern's other private label items including jams, jellies, preserves, Virginia peanuts, and Virginia wines.

generalstore@michietavern.com
(434) 977-1234

Reorder Information

*If you would like to order more cookbooks,
please contact us by phone or e-mail.*

Michie Tavern *ca.* 1784
683 Thomas Jefferson Parkway
Charlottesville, VA 22902
Phone (434) 977-1234 • Fax (434) 296-7203
E-mail address: info@michietavern.com
www.michietavern.com

Notes

Notes